Echoes of the Soul

Reflections on Life's Inner Journey

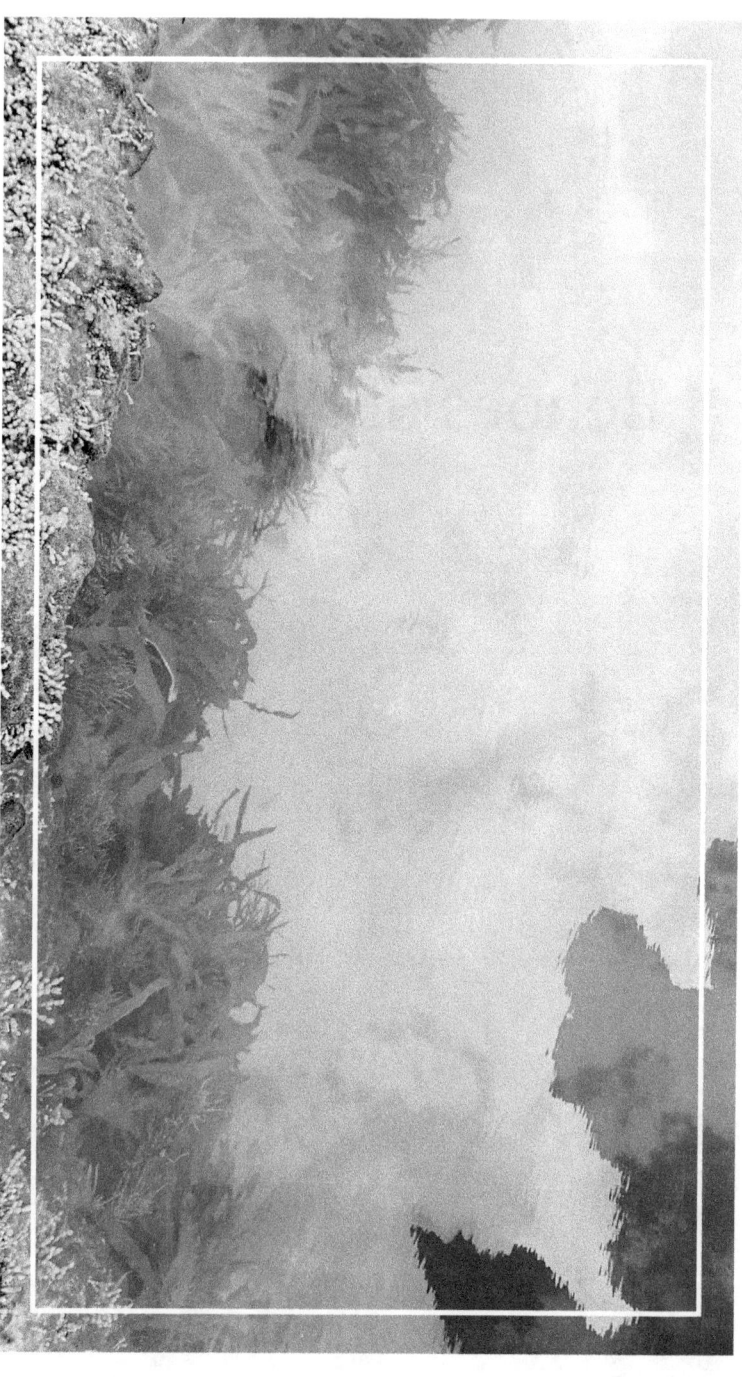

Echoes
of the
Soul

Reflections on Life's Inner Journey

BENNIE L. HANNAH

Published in Australia by Emaho Media
Postal: P.O. Box 7286, Karingal Centre, Frankston Vic 3199
Email: bhannah@netspace.net.au
Website: www.benniehannah.com

First published in Australia 2018
Copyright © Bennie L. Hannah 2018

 A catalogue record for this book is available from the National Library of Australia

National Library of Australia Cataloguing – in – Publication entry

Creator: Hannah, Bennie L., Author
Title: Echoes of the Soul: Reflections on Life's Inner Journey/
          Bennie L. Hannah
ISBN: 978-0-6481660-0-9 (Createspace paperback)
ISBN: 978-0-6481660-2-3 (epub)

Editor: Tania Brown
Cover layout and design by Didi Wahyudi
Typesetting by Cornelia Murariu at PixBeeDesign.com
Printed by Createspace

Disclaimer
All care has been taken in the preparation of the information herein, but no responsibility can be accepted by the publisher or author for any damages resulting from the misinterpretation of this work. All contact details given in this book were current at the time of publication, but are subject to change. The author and publisher shall not be responsible for any person with regard to any loss or damage caused directly or indirectly by the information in this book.

FOR MARCUS AND DANIEL,
MY SONS,
THE JOY OF MY HEART.

ACKNOWLEDGEMENTS

I gratefully acknowledge all those whose lives have embodied and shown a way along which the rest of us can follow. A way to love, a way of being Love.

I thank publishing consultant Julie Postance, for her encouragement and professional guidance in getting this book to a publishable standard.

I would like to thank Tania Brown for her editorial tuning of my manuscript, to Cornelia Murariu for her work in pulling together and providing the final touches for this beautiful book, and to Didi Wahyudi for his work on the eye-catching cover design.

Thank you to Louise Arnold for helping me to keep a 'soul' focus on the book.

I thank Catherine Fyans, Marcus Hannah, Yvonne Tserayi and Samantha Robinson whom provided valuable comments that helped guide me towards how the selections within this book would be presented.

All photos within this book were taken by myself, except for the Peruvian mountain photo (page 128) taken by Daniel Hannah, and the photo of the Angkor Wat temple in Cambodia (page 131) taken by Marcus Hannah.

Author's Note

From birth to death, with life in between,
We slowly grow into our Awakening

Echoes of the Soul is a collection of reflections about our journey through life, and Soul's journey through us. The arrangement and flow of the 101 selections contained within this book mirror these two simultaneous journeys through life, from birth to death.

These selections have a relevancy that is both immediate and eternal. They remind us that we are all in life together — that our journeys are the same yet unique. We only need to look to Nature to feel that connection with Spirit through Her.

Echoes of the Soul is told in a poetic style that speaks to hearts about the human condition. It is about our quest to find meaning and happiness in life and offers a way to see Soul's journey through the eyes of Hope and Love.

The writings in this book invite the quest for greater self-awareness, touch on the mystery of Death, and on the yearning to merge with Spirit. They point to the purpose of Soul, and to the power and beauty of Love. The early selections are about growing up, the quest to know oneself, and our search for meaning in life. Other selections are about acceptance, gratitude, the joy of living in the moment, and of Soul's growth into its Awakening.

Listen with your heart to these echoes of the Soul. I trust the selections within it will resonate with the echoes of your own Soul. The photos taken were selected to complement the writings and hopefully offer a little of the mysteriousness and beauty that can be seen in the ordinary.

Life is a blessing. There is a Nepalese greeting, 'Namaste', that roughly translates as "The god in me bows to the god in you". And so I say, Namaste!

Bennie Hannah

CONTENTS

1.

To Be Seen Just as I Stand

2.

I Sense Something Deeper

3.

I Have Chased After Wisdom

4.

Show Me How to Give

5.

I Feel You Within Me

6.

Whisperings of the Heart

7.

Guide Me to That Place

8.

Breathe Me In

9.

Echoes of the Soul

10.

I Hear My Soul Calling

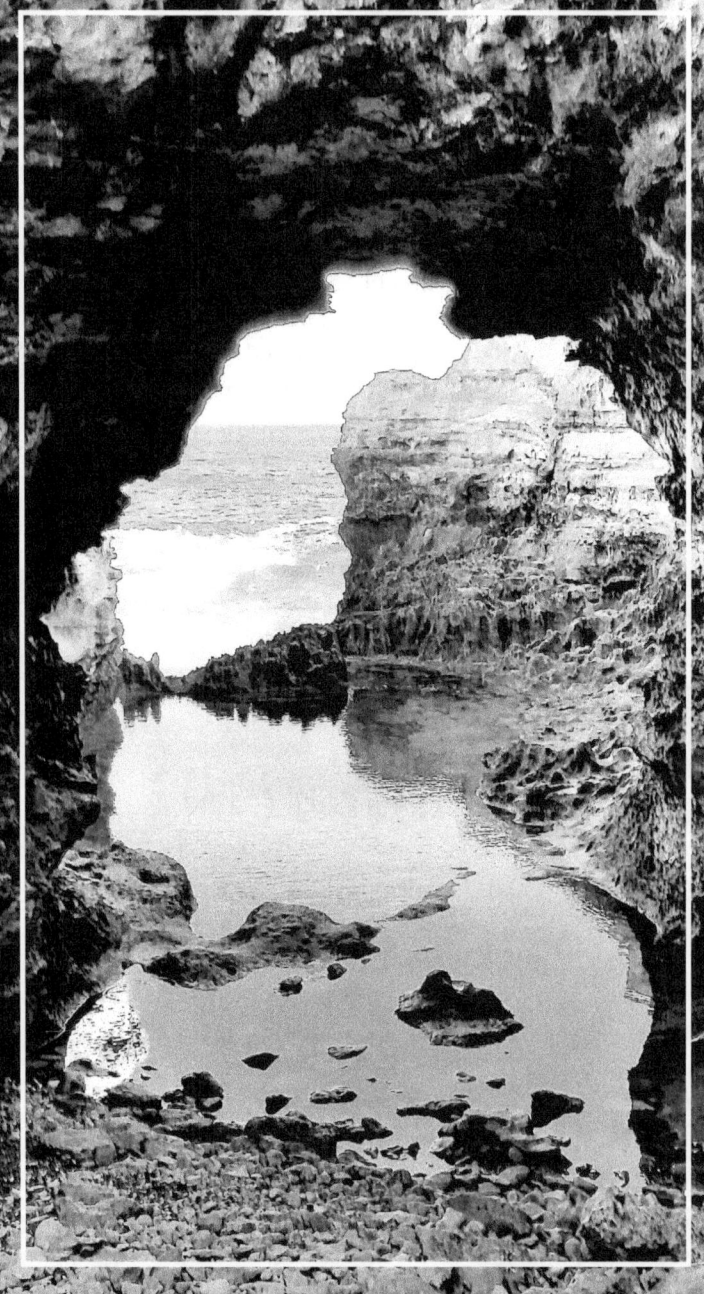

1.

To Be Seen
Just as I Stand

THE ARRIVAL

E yes unopened,
Words unformed
To define this experience
Of being born.

Yet perceiving through
A primordial sense
Discomfort of these
Quickening events,
Where body is squeezed
And forced to move,
While a rhythmic pulse
Envelops and soothes.

Through birth's release
Movement is freed.
A first breath is taken
Independently.

Now a soothing touch
While partially wiped,
As eyes behold
With blurring sight.
Then wrapped
And gently laid to rest
To hear that heartbeat
From mother's chest.

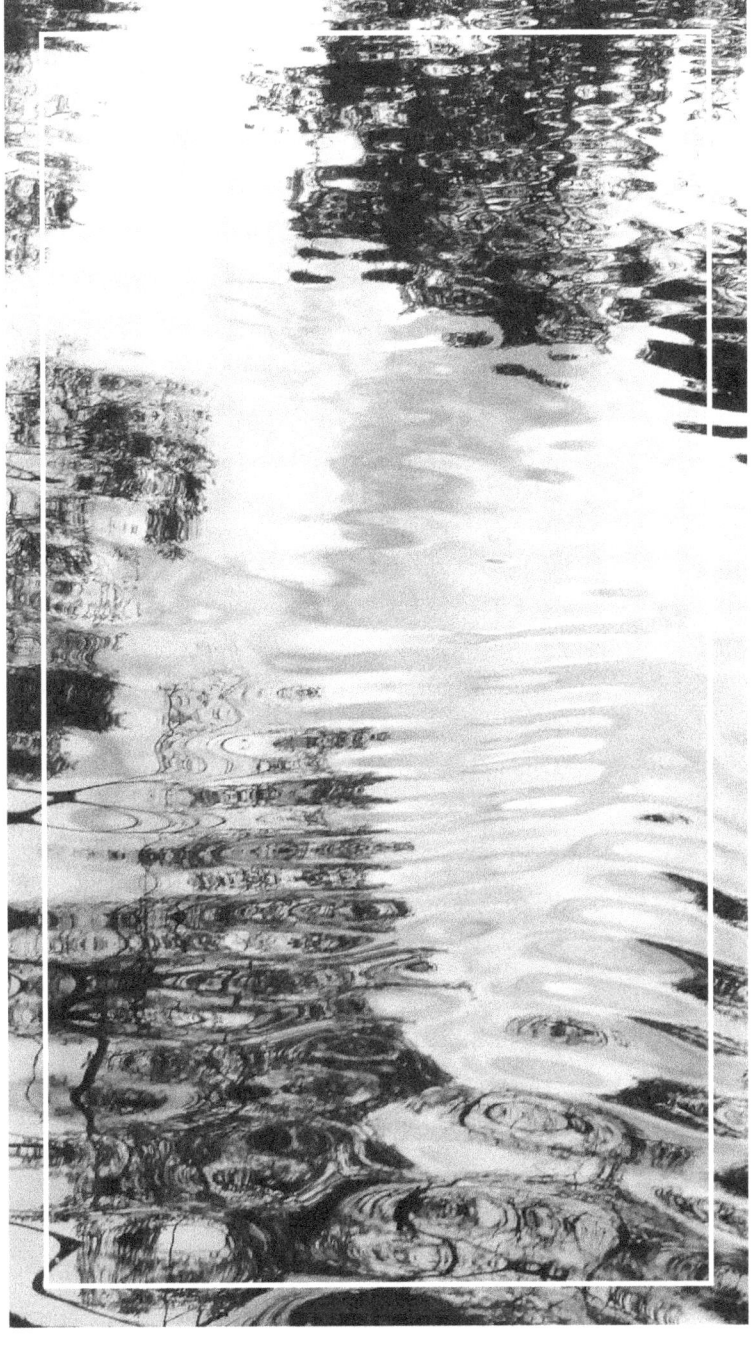

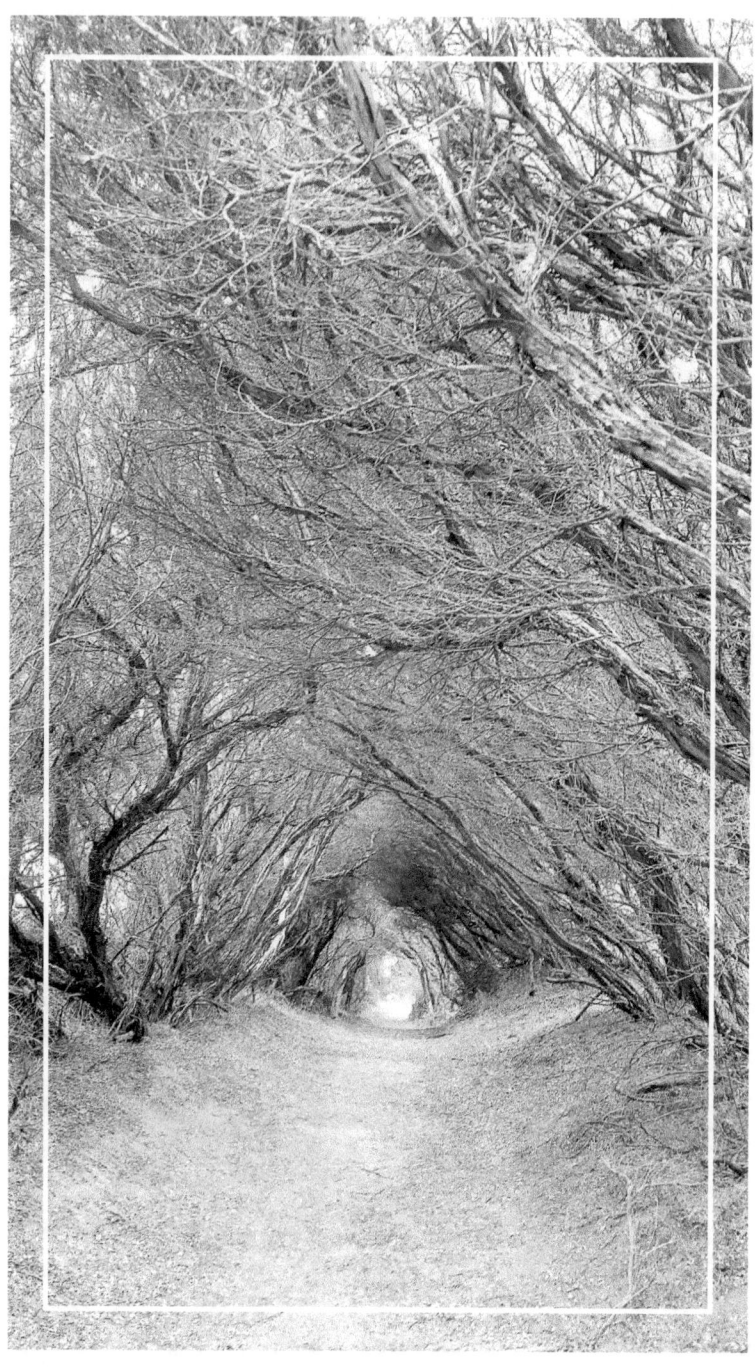

I Am Born

I am born to grow
Throughout my life until I leave it.
I am born to learn
Until my mind can hold no more.
I am born to change
The way I perceive things,
To acknowledge Life
In its simple splendor.

I am born to be free
Than to know the pain of enslavement.
I am born to be noticed,
And not have to hide.
I am born to listen
For the wisdom within the answers,
And to experience
The feelings that stir inside.

I am born to challenge
The things that limit me.
I am born to fight,
To have a sense of peace within.
I am born to hold
Onto what inspires me,
And to surrender
What my ego wants to defend.

I am born to bear the birth
Of who I am.
I am born to let my life
Unfold.
I am born to love,
That Love may fill me,
And to allow
What my life may hold.

CHILD WITH THE
FORLORN EYES

Oh, child with the forlorn eyes,
Where do you go to hide
The loneliness
That resides within your heart?

Your pain, deeply buried,
Is felt as a miscarriage
Of broken love
That you bear as a reminder
Of your yearning.

Your searching heart,
Your soulful eyes
Mark the start
Of your love's embrace,
For through your moments of doubt
You have brought about
That unrequited feeling
Without which you would not
Have been spurred on!

Quietly dwell within.
Your heart will learn
To stand alone in strength,
With Love to guide you
Through your maze of choices.

Do you sense the depth
Of your Being now?
Know somehow
That Love will gently find
A way to rest within your heart.

GROWING INTO MYSELF

Early teenage years ...
Uncertain years of growing,
Of not knowing
Who I am meant to be,
For I don't feel free
In my confusion.

Going to school
There are different rules
And forced new ways of thinking.
I am slowly learning,
Identifying what I need,
What I believe in,
And discovering feelings
Now awakening.

I've made a few friends.
I'm getting out
And doing things with them,
I'm starting to find my way.
But questions are rising
Through my searching,
And from what I'm finding ...
Questions to be answered
Another day.

Slowly I am
Growing into myself.

I Need to Find My Own Way

I need to find my own way,
To become myself,
To free the ties binding me
Under my parent's shadow.

Conflict occurs when I need help
But don't want to be saved,
For I know I need to find a way
Towards my own resolution.

When I am falling back
Into dependence,
I feel resistance arise
From knowing
I need to make my own way
In this world.

Only then can I learn
From my own mistakes
And take pride in my
Accomplishments.

Only then can I stand
On my own feet,
Greeting those I meet
And being seen as an equal.

Lost in the Moment

There's a place inside
Where emptiness resides
From my longing to share with you
A little more of me.

It is where I go when I don't know
How to express in words
Just who it is I am.

When that feeling arises within,
Telling me to flee again
From sinking into the void of deepening
Exposure,
I fear falling into the Unknown,
The depths of who I am,
To touch those places
I have resisted knowing.

It is a journey I must embrace,
Going to that place
Within,
Where inner strength
And character arise
Like a phoenix
From the ashes of Illusion.

Then I will no longer be
Lost in the moment.

To Be Seen Just as I Stand

I want to know what it is
That makes me who I am,
Unvarnished, without the paint I wear,
To be seen just as I stand.

I want to know what is inside
Filling that unseen space,
That mixture of fluidity and stagnancy
That joins me to the human race.

I cannot deny I have a will
That seems not to want to budge,
Resisting what I want to create
In the areas of my life where I'm stuck.

And I cannot deny that protective place
In the times I choose to defend,
Where my ego fights for its very life,
Though hiding in the shadows of Pretense.

I also rejoice in that place within
Where Inspiration and Creativity flow,
That respects and trusts and appreciates,
And yearns another's heart to know.

That place that wants to embrace life,
Connecting with Compassion and Joy,
That will sacrifice for a greater cause
Where my strengths I then can employ.

Yes, I want to see and feel
And to realize just who I am,
Unvarnished, with that mixture within,
To be seen just as I stand.

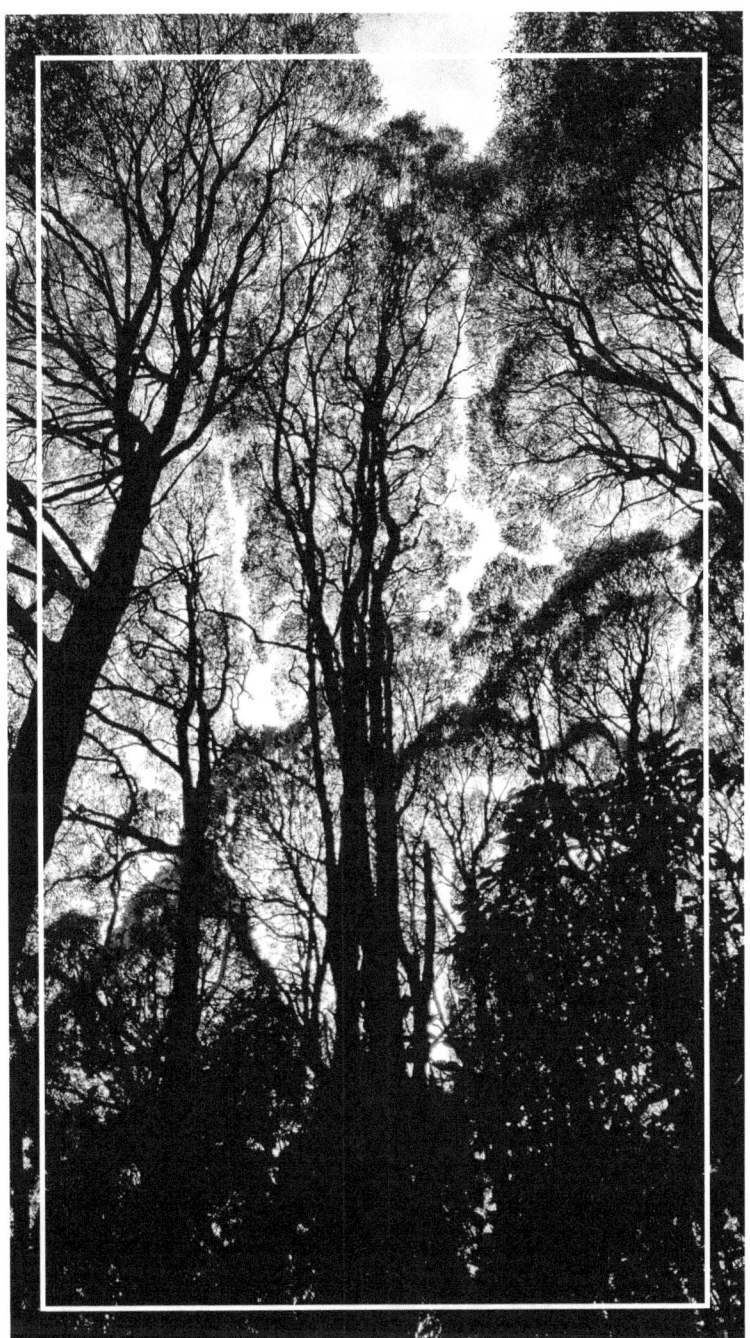

WHO AM I

Who am I,
  This one that rejects and accepts,
And believes and denies?
Who questions how to live an ordinary life?
Who forgets that with each breath I hold,
My life can only continue to unfold
By letting it go again?

When it comes to the matters
Of the mind,
Reason will limit
What intuition can define.
But the mark of my growth
Is from how I learn,
And Wisdom is something
That I must earn
Continuously.

Who am I,
This one that loves and hates,
And laughs and cries,
Who sometimes cannot see
Beyond my own eyes?
Whose myopic sight is limited by fear
Of letting others get too near
With what is still unclear
To me?

When it comes to the matters
Of the heart,
Everything I experience
Is there to play its part,
And in time I sense as my feelings grow,
My heart will tell me
What I need to know
To live freely.

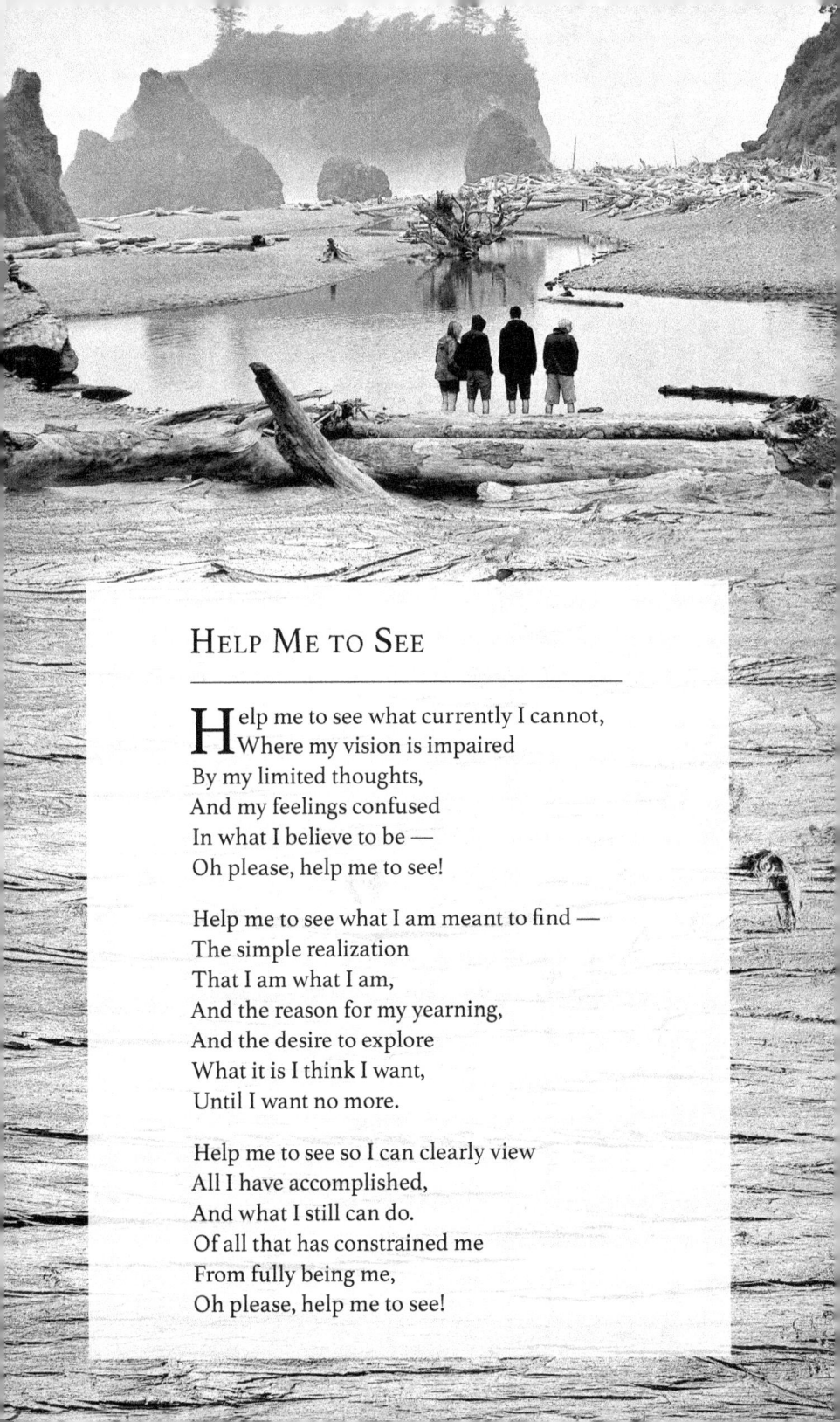

HELP ME TO SEE

Help me to see what currently I cannot,
Where my vision is impaired
By my limited thoughts,
And my feelings confused
In what I believe to be —
Oh please, help me to see!

Help me to see what I am meant to find —
The simple realization
That I am what I am,
And the reason for my yearning,
And the desire to explore
What it is I think I want,
Until I want no more.

Help me to see so I can clearly view
All I have accomplished,
And what I still can do.
Of all that has constrained me
From fully being me,
Oh please, help me to see!

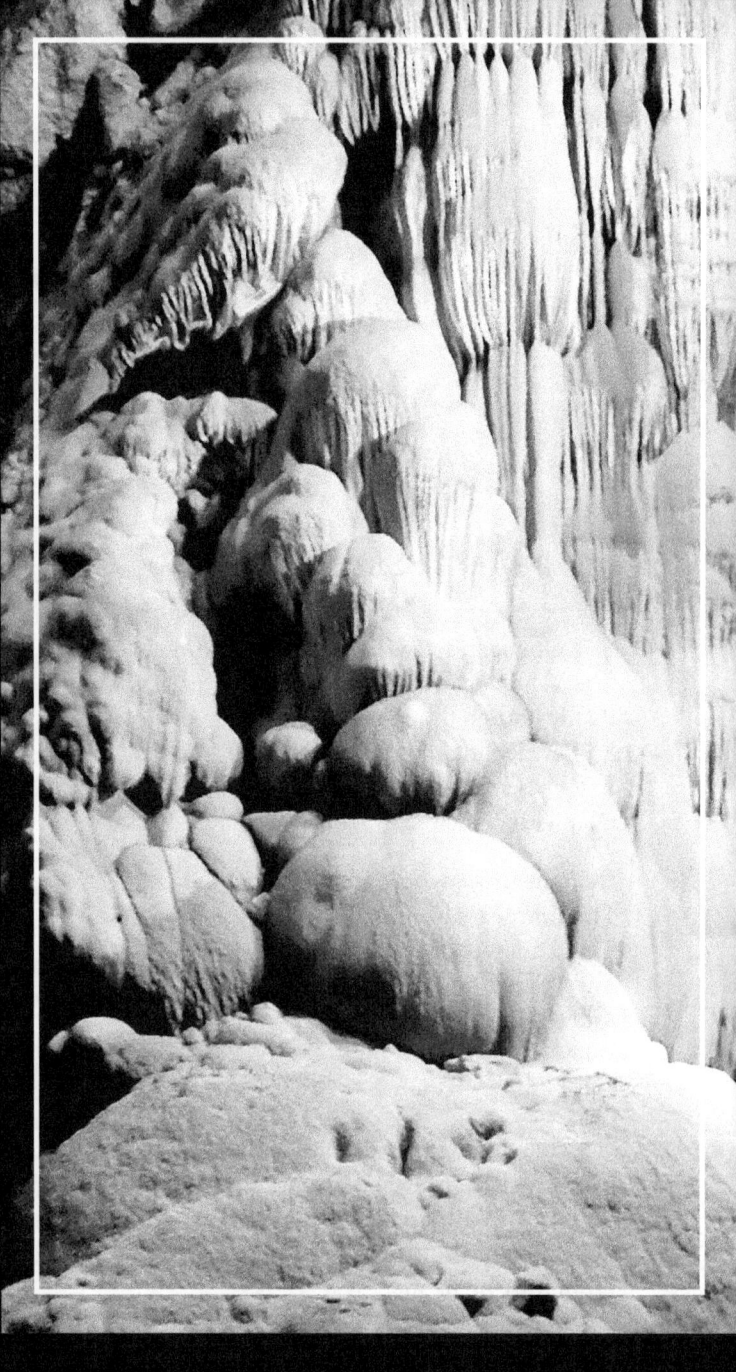

2.
I Sense
Something Deeper

I Sense Something Deeper
I Know Not Where
That Twist of Fate
I Have Walked Along That Path
Gone
Slow Down, Be in the Moment, and Connect
That I Choose to Be
Help Me to See

I SENSE SOMETHING DEEPER

My mind expands
Beyond self-constraints imposed,
With a feeling of release
And a sense of hope
That I really am more
Than what I appear to be,
For I sense something deeper,
Something that is free
Within me.

My life is challenged
In different ways.
Sometimes I forget
Who I am beneath this face,
But simple acts of love
I can share from my heart,
For I sense something deeper,
Of which I play a part.

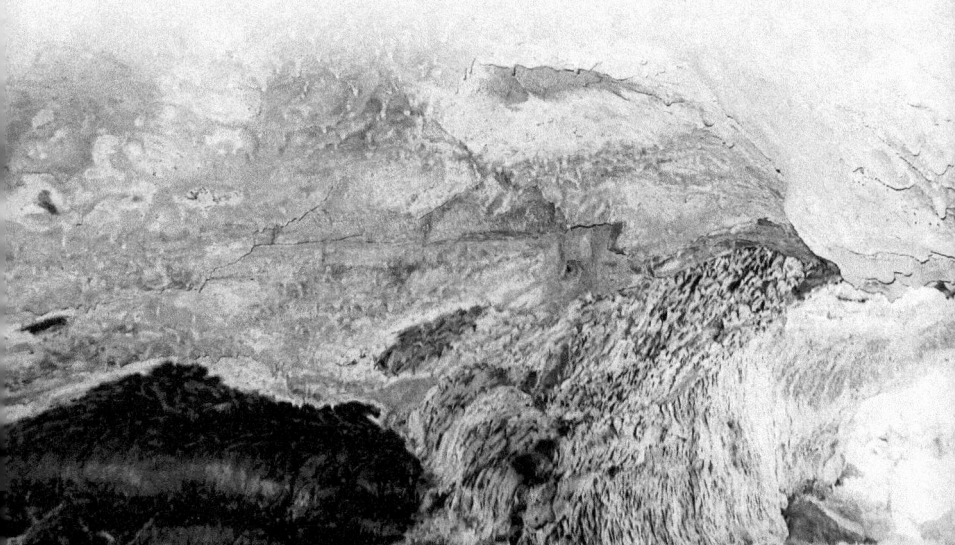

I KNOW NOT WHERE

I know not where my life will take me,
But I know I must stop resisting
An inner flow
That carries me, at times
Through rapids and over falls,
Calling me forth towards reflective pools
And along streams
Of my Becoming.

I know not where my life will end,
But in some vast sea of memory
I will merge,
Where all I have learned,
All my hopes and fears and actions
Tell the story of how I lived.

THAT TWIST OF FATE

I never saw that twist of Fate,
The one that governed
How my life played out.

While I dream of what could be,
And my desires are based on what I see,
It is somewhere between
Circumstance and Destiny
That Life in its greater majesty
Gifted me lessons to learn.

Twists do come.
I see it when I look around,
How lives are turned upside down
And right-side up,
As bridges are burned *and* made.

Life follows these twists of Fate,
The hearts and spades dealt by the Soul,
To expose those cracks
From which we grow
As we travel on our paths.

Be it Circumstance or Destiny,
Or somewhere in-between,
That twist of Fate
Forever changed my life,
Closing old doors upon my past
To force me to re-envision
Where I now want to go.

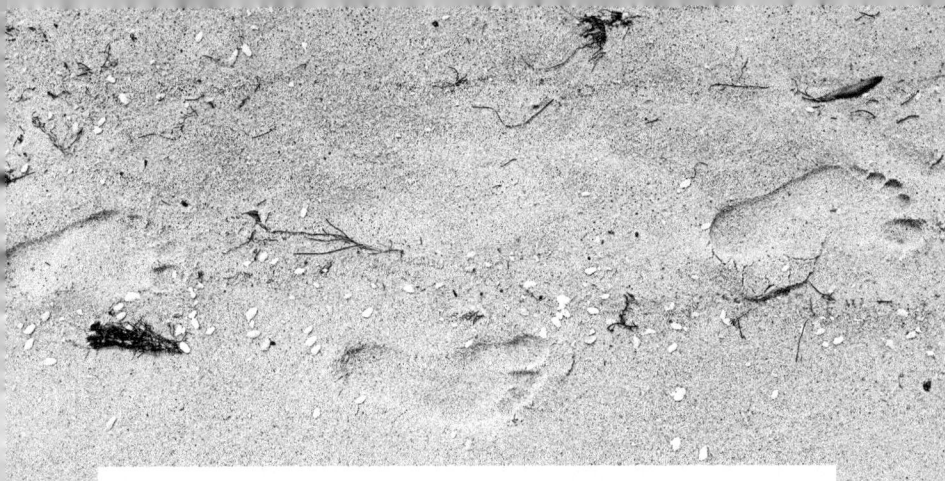

I Have Walked
Along That Path

I have walked along that path
Many times before,
Placing step after step before me,
Not sure where my journey
Would take me,
But trusting that it would lead me
To where I needed to go.

I have walked along that path
Without knowing,
Without caring
Where I was heading to,
Trying to find a few more answers
To clarify what I already knew,
But had forgotten.

As I walk along that path
Once more,
I am open to what
Is in store,
Feeling it is part of my destiny,
Though I am unsure
What will be there
At the end.

GONE

Gone are the footprints
That were washed from the sand,
That showed where I was going,
And showed where I had been.

Gone are those days,
Gone is the past,
Gone are the moments
That I knew would not last.

Gone are the journeys
That have brought me to here,
From each step I have taken,
From each thought that appeared.

Gone are the decisions,
Gone is what occurred,
Gone are the echoes
Of what now once were.

Gone, they are gone,
And tomorrow will not appear.
Never to become present,
They will always remain there.

Here, here,
This place in which I stand.
Now is the only time
In which I truly am.

SLOW DOWN, BE IN THE MOMENT, AND CONNECT

Do you see the people
Who daily pass you by,
With their momentary glances
And their audible sighs
And the busyness that dwells
Within their busy minds,
As they rush to where they're going
Even when they have the time
To slow down?

Do you hear the conversations
People around you have,
As they talk about their lives
From the viewpoint of the past
And reflect on what is missing
From what they do not have,
Rather than being
Wherever they are at
In the moment?

Do you sense the feeling,
Subtle though it be,
That lies upon
The illusive boundary
Between what we want
And what we need,
In the search to connect
With the people and the things
Around us?

Slow down, be in the moment,
And connect.
Only then will we begin
To experience
The world inside us.

That I Choose to Be

My life is given meaning
By the impulses I feel,
But it is in how I guide them
That determines if I will
Go down the path of reason,
Or where emotion beckons me,
For both can bring me to the point
That I choose to be.

At times I feel I have no control
To what occurs within my life,
But I know a choice is there
For the goals I set in sight.
I can look at my situation
Feeling entrapped by what I see,
Or I can make a move
Towards that I choose to be.

That I choose to be
Will become that which I am,
Though the reasons may be buried
Making it hard to understand.
I can surely strive to find
A path where I feel free,
For the path upon which I tread
Is the one that I choose to be.

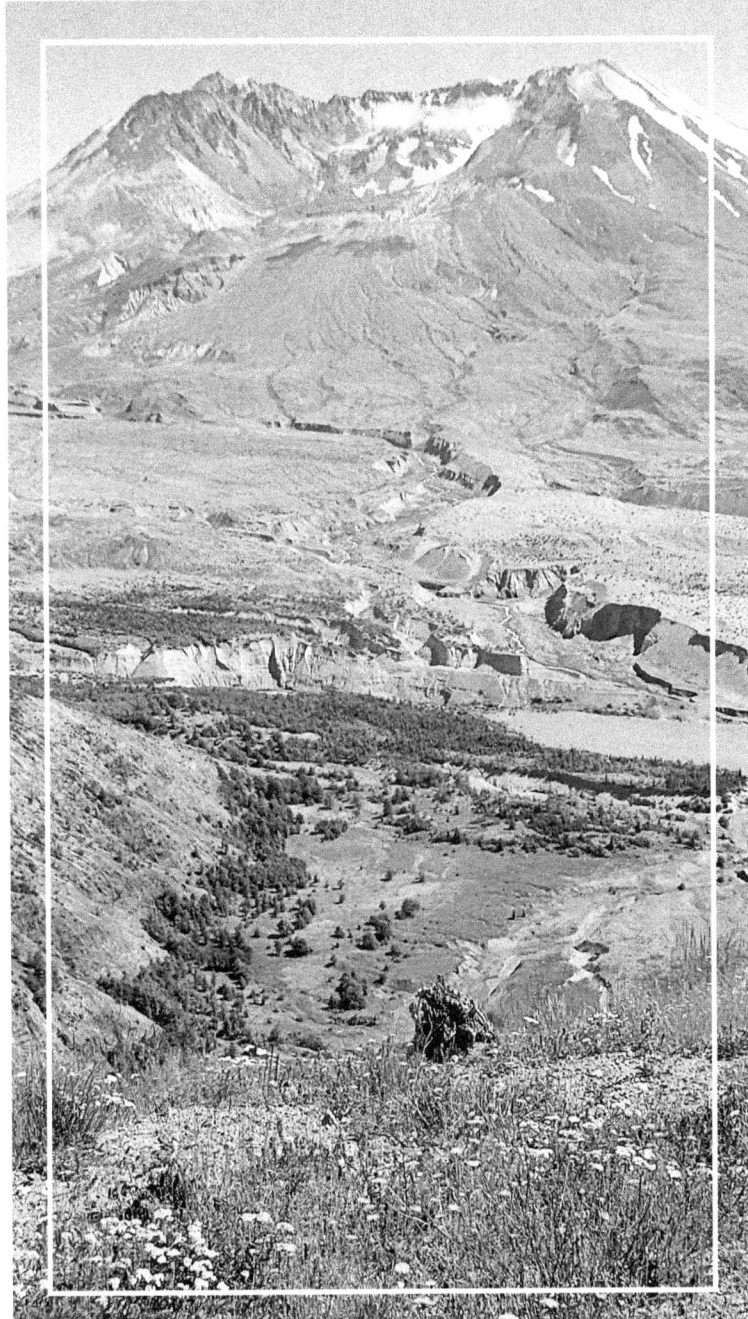

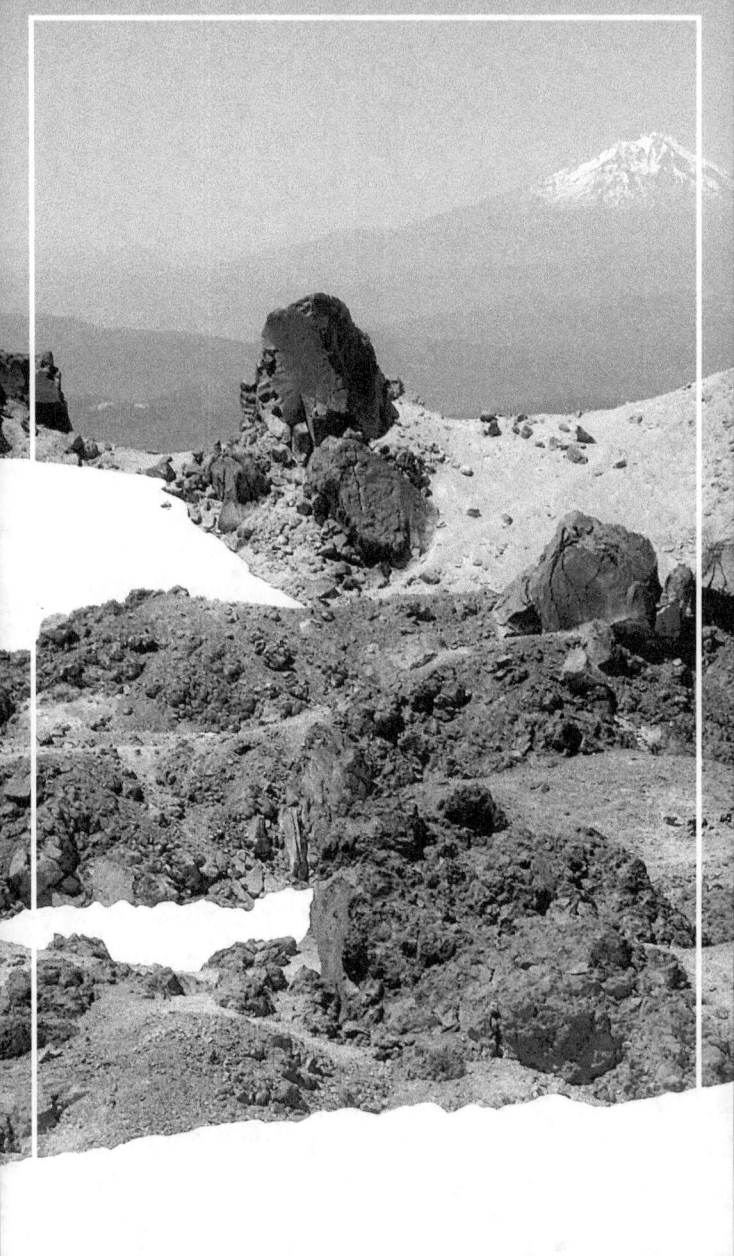

3.
I Have Chased
After Wisdom

WE LEARN LOVE

Love is given from parent to child
In selfless acts,
That we learn how
To be more selfless.

From the bonds that siblings tie,
We learn to identify Love
As being a part of family.

With friendships,
Love is found through acceptance,
Allowing Hearts to be seen
As they are,
Unmarred by pretense.

Love between lovers
Is a joining of the Hearts,
Where its fusion
Brings up all we are
To be seen.
For Love's union
Will bring up everything
Both like *and* unlike itself.

We learn Love
From those within our life,
Various forms of Love
That teach us how to be,
Helping us to see what is possible
As we open our Hearts
Unto Love's embrace.

RELATIONSHIP

Relationships are there
To create union for growth
By bringing up and exposing
All that we are.

Yet in the mirror
Of introspection
I have feared becoming too close,
Of speaking my Truth
That would develop trust
With you, and within myself.

In opening up,
In learning about you
And letting you know about me,
I honor the growth
Of our journeys.

For our life paths are guided
By how we relate
To the people we meet
And the friendships we make,
Both as we come,
And as we go on our
Own way.

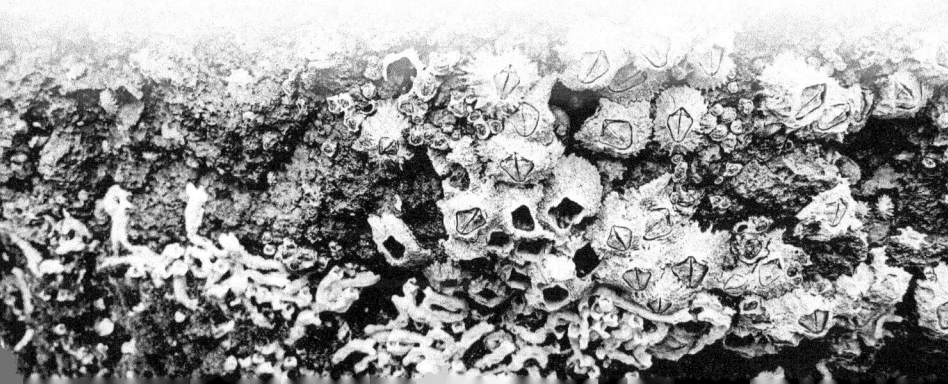

Yet I Know You Not

I know you,
Yet I know you not.

We shared years
Together,
Dreamt, laughed,
Voiced our fears
And wept
In each other's arms.

When the dreams
Ended,
We parted ways,
Mindful of the bonds
We had,
And those that
Remained.

When I forgot
That I know you not,
I forgot to appreciate
The unfolding Mystery
Of who you were
Becoming
Each day.

Love's joy
Was in my exploration
Of your journey
To know
Yourself.

THE VOICES I CARRY

The future is governed
By the past,
The living governed
By the dead.
I need to stop listening
To the voices in my head.

To the ghosts of society
And of my ancestors too,
Voices that define my conscience,
Defining both me and you.

It is only by being
More conscious,
Knowing what is real,
That I can ever be true to myself,
Aligned with what I feel.

More will be expected
As I listen to Freedom speak,
For as I live my own life
I assume its responsibility.

I then become responsible
For how I am living in the world,
When the voices I carry
Are no longer there to rule.

LOVE'S OPPORTUNITY DENIED

If I love
From the fullness of my Being,
And act
From the fullness that this brings,
There would be no regrets
Nor opportunities lost,
And no love denied
With its heart-felt cost.

There would be no conflicts
From the wounds incurred
When I only half live
And only half learn.
For conflict will not arise
To take root within
When I am not living
A contradiction.

Life shows me
Where I withhold from myself,
As grief over another
Is not grief for someone else.
The pain that deeply hurts
Is Love's opportunity denied
From expressing my Being
And the fullness of my life.

Loss *in* Love is not the same
As loss *of* Love,
That leaves me feeling incomplete
Within my Love.
For if I connected
From the fullness of my Being,
Joy, not grief
Will remain!

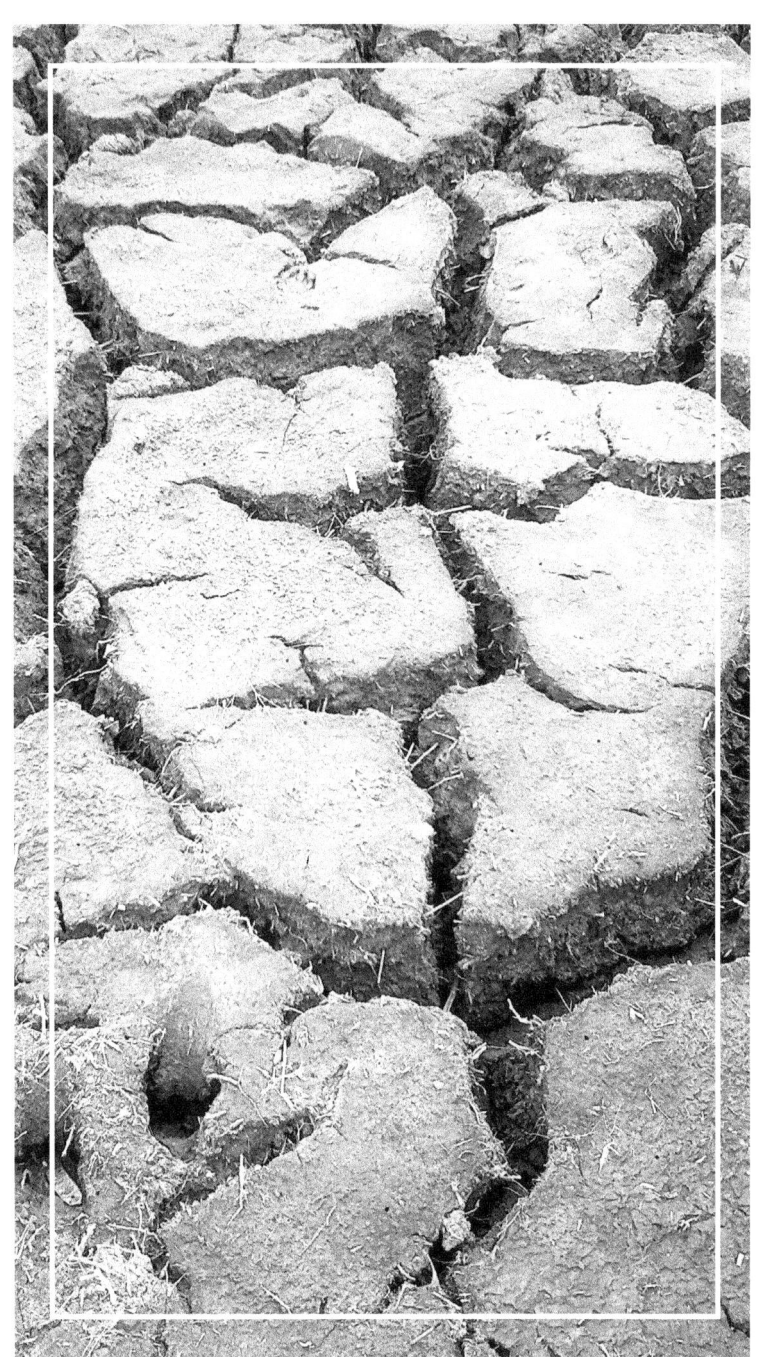

I HAVE THOSE DAYS

I have those days
When I feel like I have
Fallen from grace,
When my life lies in shambles
And I wonder how I reached
That state of being.

With prayer and curses
I stumble along
Until I reach the void of Silence,
A place that holds
And gently lifts me
Into self-acceptance.

I have those days
When I realize I am okay
No matter how I am,
As I learn to see myself
From within,
Speaking my Truth,
And rising to meet the challenges
That confront me.

I have those days
Where I feel anything is possible!
When I realize
I cannot be contained,
Then Joy and Freedom
Will be mine.

PLEASE HEAR MY HEART

Please hear my Heart
For I know not what to say,
As words escape me
At the moment.
I wait here yearning
To know You,
Feeling alone without You,
Like the night must feel
When the moon does not shine.

As when the night is dark
The stars appear brighter,
So all the little things
That bring me joy and laughter
Are because I know You are there
Even in times of my darkness.

Please hear my Heart
That yearns to know Your Love.
Yet why do I turn away
To walk lonely streets
Filled with the desires of Illusion,
That only throws my mind
Into confusion
From not finding You?

Please hear my heart
And gently guide me back to Thee,
That I may know peace
From not searching.

LOVE NEEDS NOT BELIEF

Love needs not Belief
For its beauty to be seen
Within the hearts
Of those who love,
And in the minds
Of those who dream.

Love does not need Belief
For its power to be felt,
As a stirring of the desire
To extend beyond the Self.

It needs not Belief
For its voice to be heard
As a song upon our lips,
Or an inner whisper.
Nor does it need Belief
For it to be understood,
For its joy to be experienced
And offered in Gratitude.

Love needs not Belief
In words it must transcend,
For Love that touches
Hearts and Souls
Has no beginning,
It has no end.

Please Be With Me

Please be with me
As I strive to understand
The delicately poising mystery
That confronts me once again.

Where echoes of Love's promise
Reverberate within,
As I listen to Your whisperings
Carried on the wind.

Please be with me
As I go upon my quest
To discover what it is
That I need to address,
As I learn to embrace
Both the shadows and light
That creates its varied hues
On the canvas of my life.

Please be with me
Until Your Joy does come,
When my Heart has learned to merge
Beyond this separate one.

I Have Chased After Wisdom

I have chased after Wisdom
And sought to grab Her hand,
Yet when I thought I was getting close
I was left behind again.
For everything I hear and read
Still does not satisfy
A deeper urge to know myself
That Knowledge cannot define.

My Ego tries to make me think
Knowledge means Wisdom too,
But Knowledge devoid of experience
Cannot show me what is true.
For my experiences are the only thing
That others cannot deny,
While Knowledge has its ebbs and flows
Along the course of Time.

How can I know what is true
If I do not question what I believe?
Yet confusion continues to rule my mind
When thoughts are left to breed.
Thus I try to look within
To see what Is without,
At which time the knowledge I have
Matters not, somehow.

From this point I can then reflect
From a different way of Seeing,
And Wisdom I hope would take my hand
To live a different way of Being.

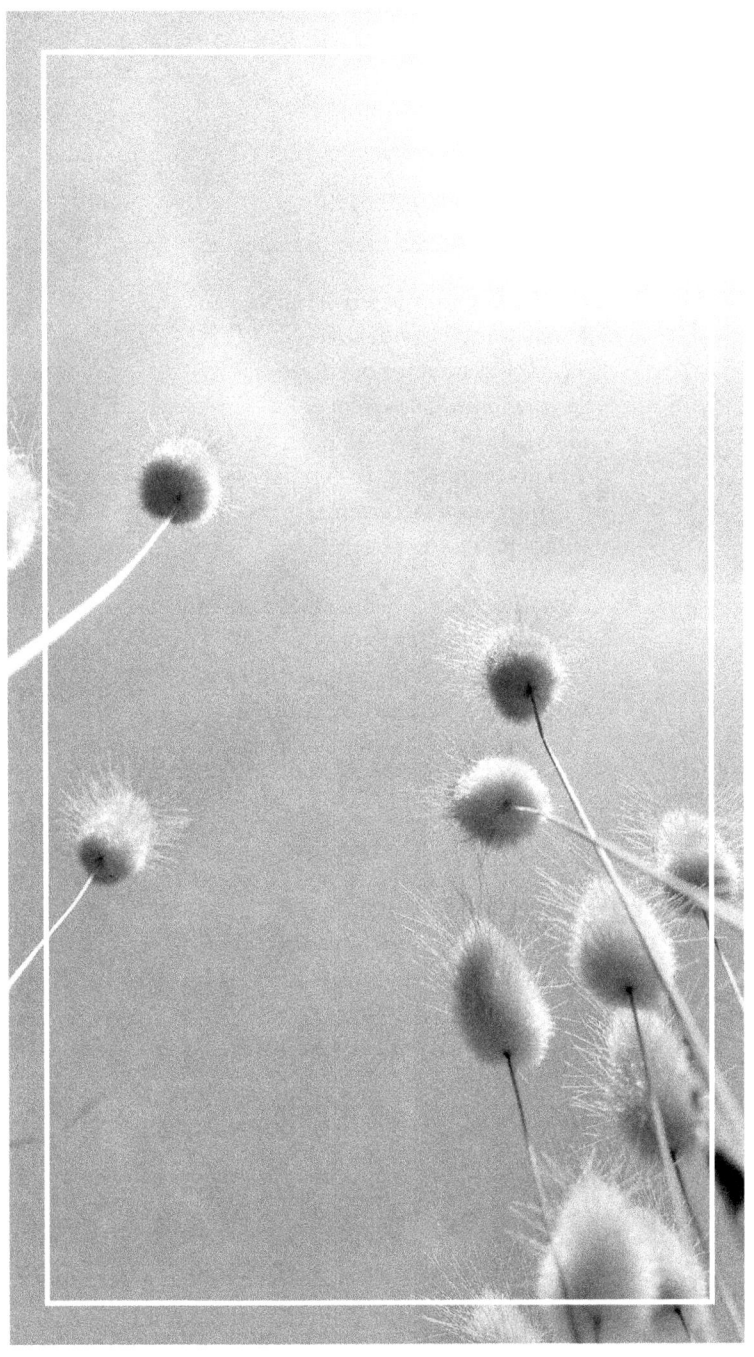

THE QUESTIONS

In the moment before Time began
In a point without space,
A cataclysmic force occurred
Setting motion into place.
Thus was this universe born
And now continues to expand,
Raising questions science finds
Difficult to understand.

How did Consciousness first appear?
It is not limited as I know.
Where began those blueprint designs
From which all forms unfold?
How does Love propel one to care
For strangers they have only met,
And what visions do the mystics see
In that state of altered bliss?

How do we explain miracles
That science has no answers for?
Could we be part of a dream
In the mind of a Cosmic Lord?
What happens to time when we let go
Of our future and our past,
And how do we explain Life
If these questions we do not ask?

GRIST FOR THE MILL

A question to be asked
Is an answer to be found.
But knowledge is not Wisdom
If Ignorance hangs around,
So down throughout the Ages
The Sages have implied
That Truth is but a fallacy
If its basis is a lie.

As we look more closely
At this life that we create,
We see within our thoughts
What some may call our fate.
For as we think we do believe
Until we change our view,
And thus, for change to occur
We need to see anew.

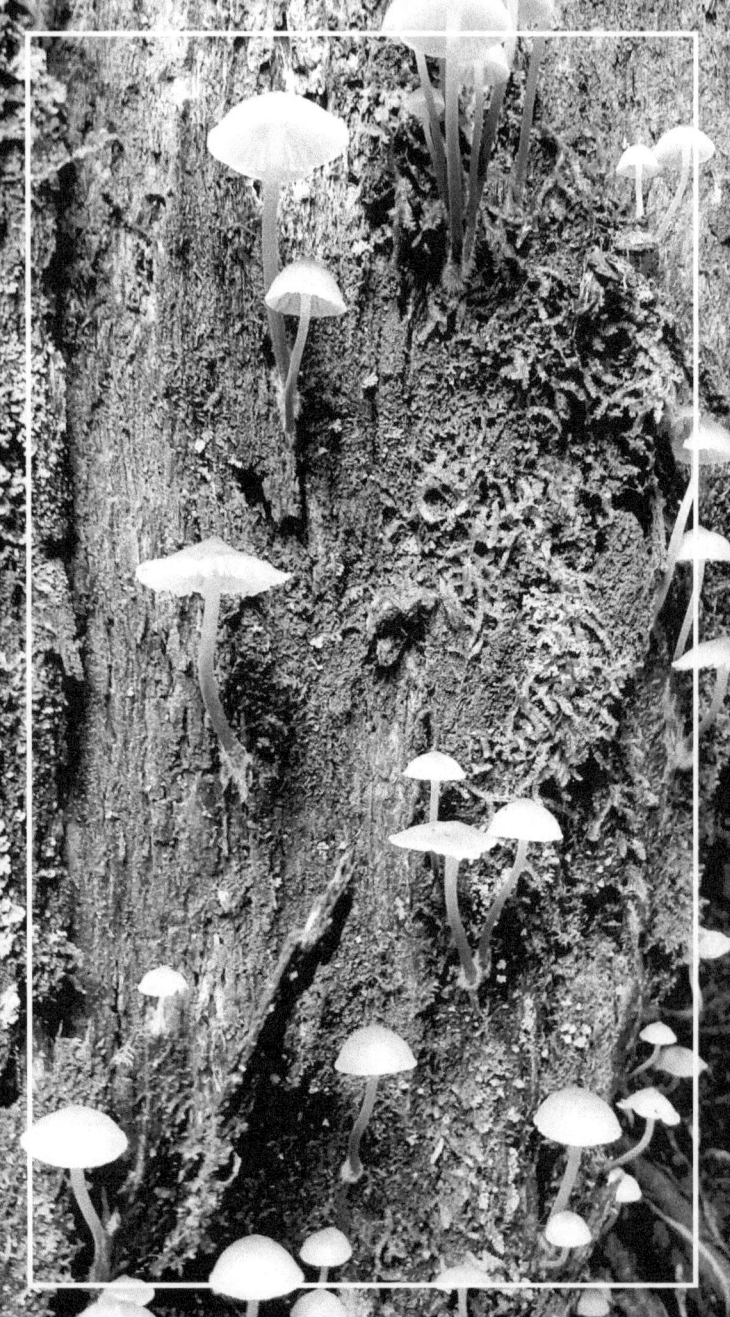

4.

Show Me
How to Give

How Colorless Would Be the World
It Is a Small World
There Is a Song We Must Sing
If There Were Only One Way
What Will Be Left Behind
Show Me How to Give
I Love the Wild Places
Metamorphosis
Life Is How I Can Give
Coming Back to Now
Presence

How Colorless Would Be the World

How colorless would be the world
If it were only black and white?
How bland would taste the food
If it weren't for the spices?

How muted would it seem
If it weren't for all the sounds,
And how lonely would we feel
If we had no one around?

How much would we miss
If the scents we could not smell?
How blind would we be
If our Wisdom began to fail?

How would be societies
If not for the different faiths?
And how would we find our world
If it lacked its different races?

It Is a Small World

The oceans are vast
And the mountains high,
The deserts imposing
With dunes hot and dry.
Dense forests and grasslands
Stretch across the globe,
While the tundra and glaciers
Seem inhospitable.

Large cities and small villages
Lie far, far apart,
While cultures and religions
Speak to different hearts.
But when we look more broadly
Then we start to see
It is a small world.

When we view this world
From deep in outer space,
We see just how
Precious is this place,
Yet greed and power
Have distorted our view
To the point that this world
We have sadly abused.

It limits our remembering
That people are the same,
That we bleed, we love,
And we often fear change.
The time has come now
Our differences to mend,
To see it is a small world.

There Is a Song We Must Sing

There is a song we must sing,
One we learned since time beginning.
We have forgotten many of the words
And await reminding what we heard
So long ago.

It is a song about Life and how we live,
And will lead us to that place within
That tells us how we came to be,
Showing us what we need to see
Around us.

Our song is what we need to convey
To express ourselves, as we create
A way in which we can understand
The contrasts that appear within
Our lives.

It is a song only we can hear
As we heed the voice of Love, not Fear.
For the tune we subtly feel
Defines what we know is real
And what is not.

Our song is there for us to sing
As we remember who we are being.
It contains the melody of our life
That we will sing until that time
It becomes us.

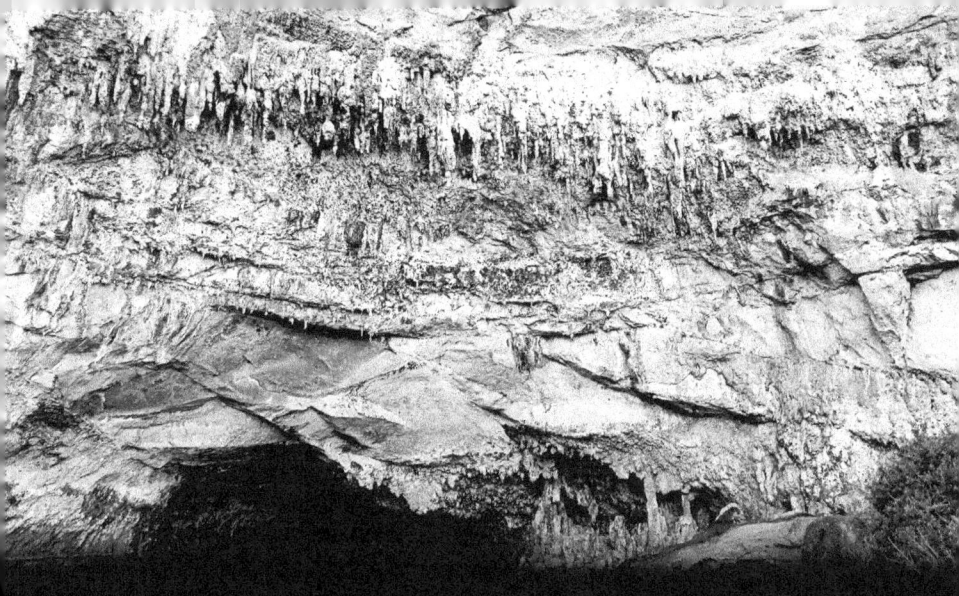

If There Were Only One Way

If there were only one Way,
One path to Heaven's door,
One key to access there,
Then how would Life be fair?

Differing cultures
Have differing beliefs,
Yet their wise men all agree
The Heart itself
Is what must lead.

Compassion is born there,
And Justice raised.
These are what point the Way.
Only then can we progress
Towards Wisdom and Love itself.

If there were only one Truth,
One way to see the world,
If Life did not lead us there,
Then how would life be fair?

What Will Be Left Behind

What will be left behind
That will define
Who I am and what I was?

What traits displayed
Portray the sum of me
Beyond my accomplishments
And failures?

Of those who knew me,
What did they see?
What fragments of my identity?

What will be left behind
That I can find
Has given my life meaning,
Of knowing in some way
I touched the life of others?

What in turn have I learned
That I can teach another
From my attempt to understand
This Mystery that I am?

SHOW ME HOW TO GIVE

Show me how to give,
That my giving is from my Heart
And not from my Mind.
Then will I feel
The true joy of giving
As a loving expression
Of Life.

Show me how to live,
That my life is imbued
With the thought of You
From dawn to dusk.
Life will then feel complete,
As I seek to be one
With Your love.

Show me how to love,
Love that is without restraint,
Love not contained by fear,
So that throughout the years,
I will remember how
To give of myself.

I Love the Wild Places

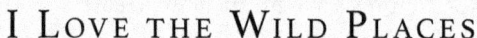

I love the wild places,
For they calm and soothe
My restless soul,
Connecting me
With some inner place,
An untamed space within,
Perhaps my journey's end
When I learn
To stop yearning.

I love the wild places
Unfettered by Life's desire,
Shaped and tempered
Through their surrounds,
Yet defiant as they remain
Unbound
And unmasked,
Changeless
Yet eternally changing
As the past
Merges into the future.

Forever shall I love
The wild places!

METAMORPHOSIS

I sense that subtle urge
To expand beyond the self,
So I learn to define myself
In ever-changing ways.

Change is Life,
And growth is change,
Whether from exalted joy
Or the deepest pain.
Each moment's birth
Is another's death,
So I need to surrender unto it
Without regret.

Stagnation is the death of Soul,
Thus will Soul remind me
When I need to know
Once more.

Life will find me
And Death will greet me,
Both playing their part
To dissolve the self
So that the Self is known!

It is only through my own
Metamorphosis
I can be free to fly away
On the winds of change.

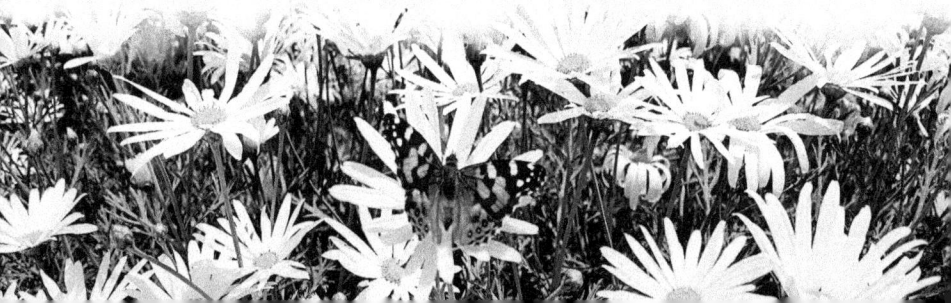

LIFE IS HOW I CAN GIVE

I would like to hold onto
The things I know,
But Time will make me
Let them go.

So as I look at how I live,
I am beginning to realize
Life is not about what I have,
But how I can give.

It is in the opportunities
To share who I am,
To touch another's life
In whatever way I can
That will define for me the joy
Of a life well lived,
For then I can say
Life is not about what I have,
But how I can give.

COMING BACK TO NOW

I have been off on a journey
Lasting for days,
Taking me to places
Far and wide,
Places lived inside my mind.

It is a strange thing
When I am dreaming
While I am awake,
Thinking but not realizing
The state I am in,
Sleepwalking
Through a world of thoughts,
Of times that have been
Or that could be.

It was in the moment
Of remembering,
Of feeling my breath
And my feet upon the ground,
That I could appreciate once more
The simple beauty of Being.

PRESENCE

I walk in the brisk winter air,
Trying to be present with where
I am in the moment.

It is such a simple thing,
Yet hard to do,
For the mind is not like a tool
That easily settles into the groove
Of compliance.

Yet, when I focus on the sound
Of a chorus of frogs,
My mind comes around
To listen,
Intrigued by a stillness
Within the moment.

Becoming deeply absorbed,
I seem to dissolve
Into the void of Awareness,
Where the space separating
Me from it also dissolves.

For one freeing moment,
I am within a space
Devoid of thought.

Losing my focused attention,
My mind once again
Grants me distractions,
For as long as I am willing
To be distracted.

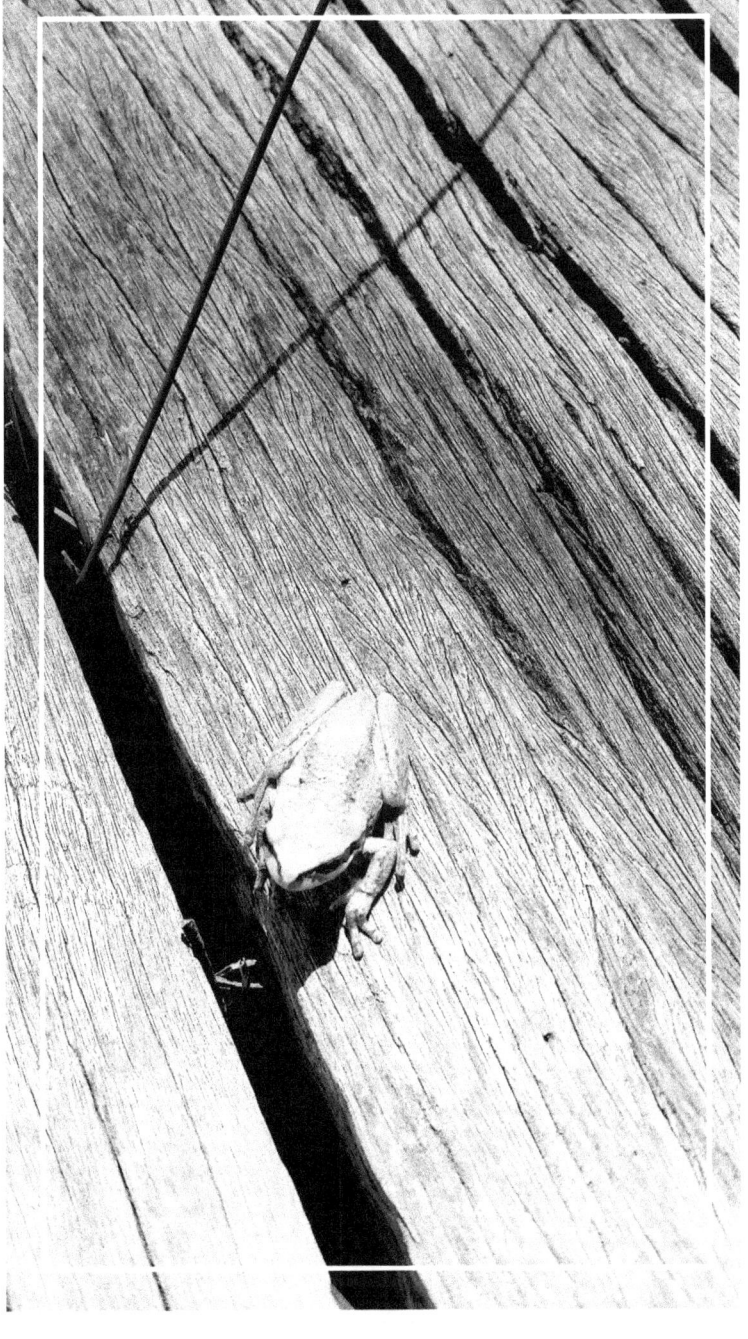

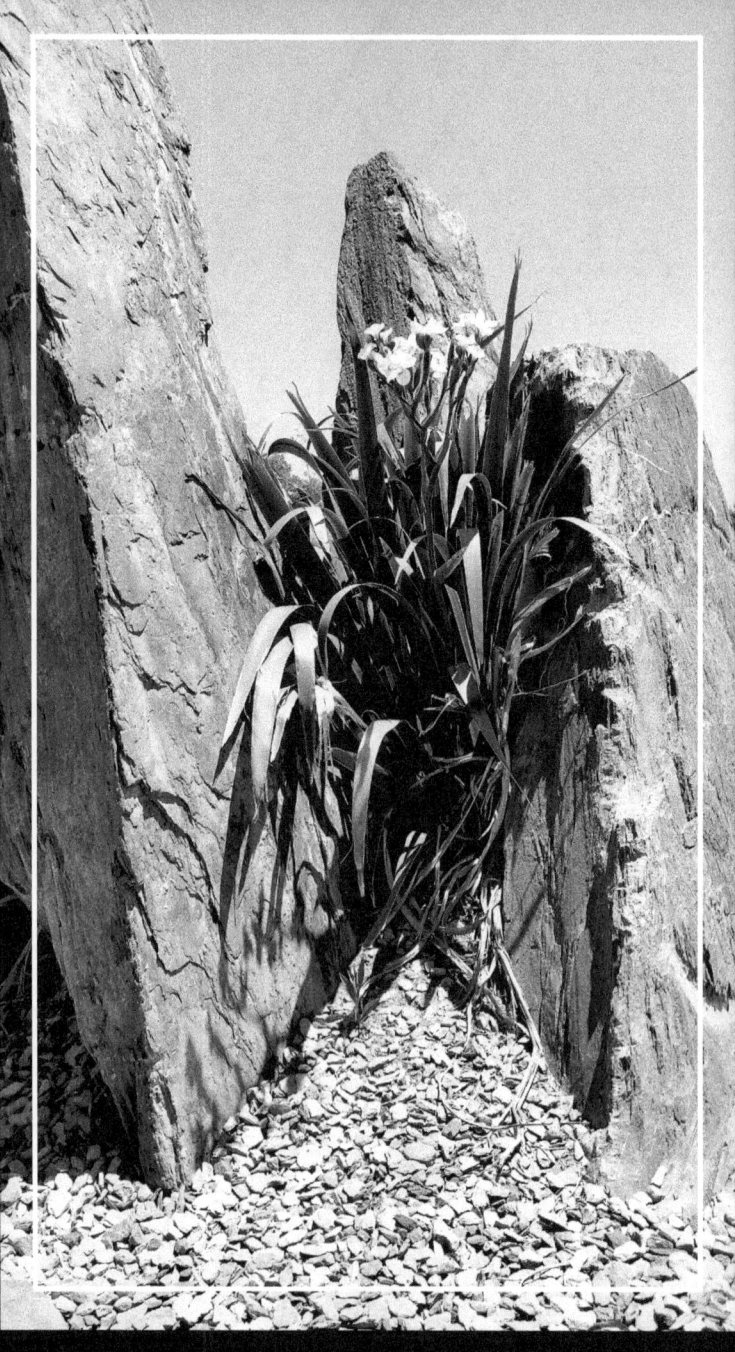

5.

I Feel You Within Me

As I Listen to You Sing
I Feel You Within Me
The Purpose of the Word
Let Peace Be Me
It Is Those Simple Things
Each Day
In That Mysterious Place
Life Cannot Be Rushed
I Find Another Reason
In Those Moments of Joy
Something Stirs Deeply

As I Listen to You Sing

I am transformed in this moment
As I listen to you sing,
As you take me to a place
Of greater yearning,
Where my Soul rises upon
The wings of Love
To merge for a moment
In that transcendent feeling
Of unfettered Joy.

There is an ineffable quality
To how you sing,
As you gently bring yourself
Closer to your heart,
From which you are able
To impart
Your love's embrace.

I yearn to be one
With the words you sing,
For in them
I hear you rejoicing
Unrestrained.

As you fall silent
I am transformed once again
Within that stillness,
Aware of having been filled
By the fullness of Love.

I Feel You Within Me

Wherever I go, wherever I am,
Whatever I do, whatever I've done,
No matter how slow or fast that I run,
I feel You within me.

As its colors are to a painting,
As its lines are to a drawing,
As the picture is to the framing,
I feel You within me.

You are there
And comfort me in my pain,
Like the sun that shines
Even while it is raining.
I dream now
And see a better way
For I feel You within me.

As near as the breath I take,
As close as the thoughts I think,
As are the words that I speak,
I feel You within me!

THE PURPOSE OF THE WORD

Down throughout the Ages
The voice of Wisdom has been heard,
To impress upon the mind of Man
The purpose of the Word.

With each unfoldment of a Truth divine
That aligns with our inner eye,
We gain a glimpse of how to live
As we journey within this life.

How can we think the Mind of God
Is limited to our beliefs,
To one set way that all must pray
While we ignore diversity?

For underlying the richness of
The way our Souls evolve,
The purpose of the Word
Is what our hearts must learn to solve.

LET PEACE BE ME

As I look upon this world diverse,
I see Nature has, over Time's course,
Found balance through its myriad forms
In the places that support them.

Now look at Man, with mind supreme,
Who can create a life to reflect his dreams
But somewhere along the way,
Has forgotten what the Elders say.

For we cannot ignore this life,
Nor offer war as a sacrifice
For Peace, then pretend we do not see
That another way is what we need.

We must learn to rise above our past,
Allowing our differences to heal at last,
For if we truly want Peace to be,
Then we must say "Let Peace be me".

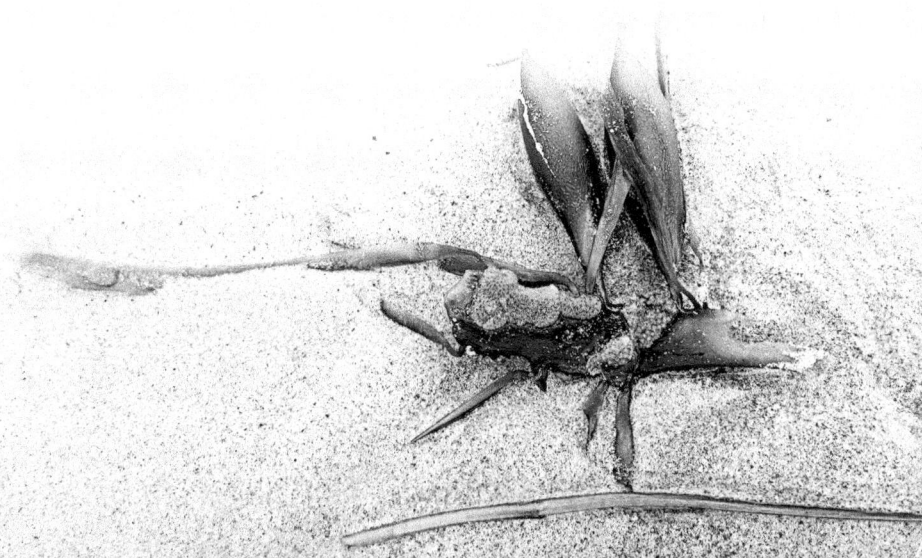

IT IS THOSE SIMPLE THINGS

It is those simple things
That soothe and stir my Soul.

From the notes of a piano
To the gurgling of a brook ...
Of a prolonged look
With a smile of surprise,
And in wizened eyes
That have seen the years.

It is in the tears of a child
Being soothed.
In the ring of Truth
Within an answer I hear,
Or the courage to face a fear
To realize a dream.

It is those simple things ...

From the bonds between
Family and friends.
In the engaging conversations
Between two hearts,
To the relief pouring forth
When disaster unites us.

It is in joy expressed
And a quietened mind,
To the peace I find
When in Nature's fold ...

Yes, it is those simple things
That soothe and stir my Soul.

EACH DAY

Each day my life begins anew.
Each day I have a chance to choose,
A choice to make,
In what it is that I may give,
In what it is that I may take.

Each day I awake I know I'm blessed,
Each day! Though I fall into forgetfulness,
Into old routines,
In how it is I see the world,
In how it is the world may seem.

Each day I need to take a pause,
I need to reflect on how I'm called,
On what I've done, on what I'll do,
On what makes me 'me'
And what makes you 'you'.

And then I may awake with Grace,
With gratitude this day to face.

Each day I have a little more time.
Each day there is something I can find,
A way to give,
That honors my life and who I am,
That reflects this time in which I live.

IN THAT MYSTERIOUS PLACE

In that mysterious place where Beauty is felt,
We dip into the pool where Ego melts
Momentarily,
A place where our perceptions are clear
Without mind to analyze what is there,
Nor to judge.

For in the simple array of a flower,
And the gurgling of a stream, as we watch the water
Pass by,
There unfolds an essence of who we are,
An undefinable connection with nature
That fills us.

In that mysterious place where Love occurs,
We open up to reach out beyond our own hurts
To another.
Its wings carry us into regions of our heart
We may have thought departed,
Not to return.

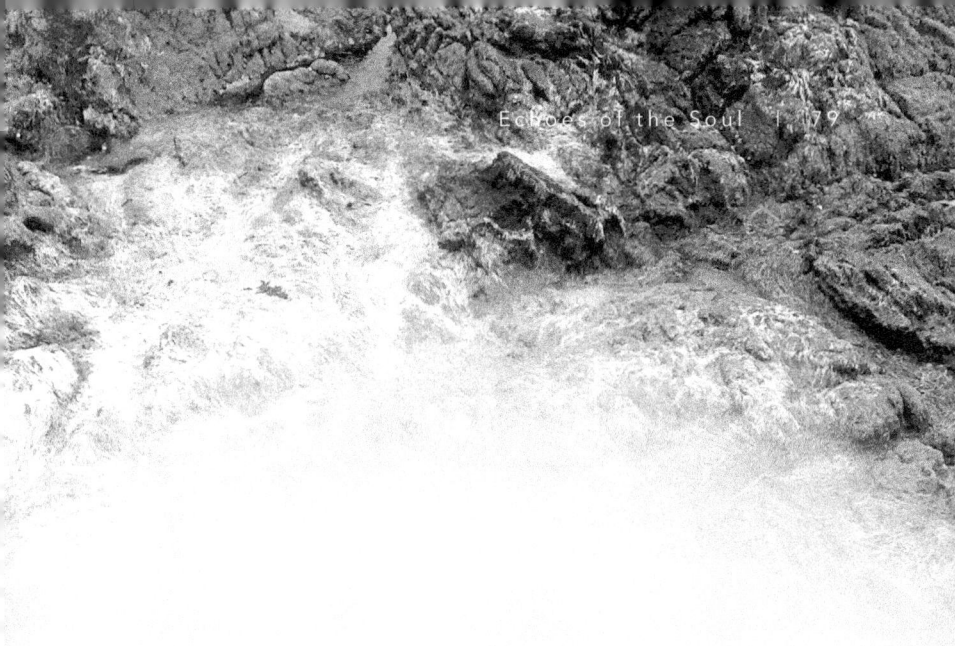

For in the connection with what we feel,
Pretense falls away to reveal
Our love unfettered.
For Love is expansion of light into the dark,
To illumine that path upon which our heart
Travels.

In that mysterious place where Life unfolds
To form both the known and unknown,
We become.
Our lives evolve, our awareness too.
We live to love and grow from what we knew
Before.

For in the simple flow of Life
There is no wrong, there is no right
We must choose between.
All our experiences point to the time
When we are able to define our self
As Love expressed.

LIFE CANNOT BE RUSHED

Life is not fortuitous,
And I know it cannot be rushed,
Nor are lessons gleaned
Through Wisdom's eyes
Compressed into a moment.

Life cannot be rushed
When Patience and Tolerance and Trust
Are being developed within it.

These will come in time,
As Time itself expands and unfolds
As another aspect of Soul
From which to develop.

Joy and Love also cannot be forced,
But are reflections of the heart's choice
To open unto Life.

With the passage of time,
As Soul arises from its worldly confines,
Why should its lessons stop
When unfettered by form?
For if born in the image of Love,
Would not the lessons in Love
Continue?

I FIND ANOTHER REASON

From the heights of possibility
To the lows of when I've crashed,
Through the maze of my life's options
To the clarity I gain at last,
I find another reason
That tells me why I'm here,
As I live to face the moments
Between my courage and my fears.

From the daily routines I live
To the adventures I am on,
Through the quest to find fulfillment
To the loss of what is gone,
I find another reason
Between the future and my past,
That promises me comfort
With being where I'm at.

From the worries that beseech me
To the peace that sometimes comes,
Through the voice of my conscience
My life is largely run,
Still I find another reason
As I look for missing clues,
That helps me make more sense
Of what I thought I knew.

IN THOSE MOMENTS OF JOY

In those moments of Joy
When I am just glad to be alive,
I can appreciate how I am
When I do not feel confined.

For I realize in those moments,
Though my mind may digress,
That my heart has the power
In simplicity to rest.

I can look at a cloud
Or the mud upon my shoe,
And in that moment of acceptance
I can offer my gratitude.

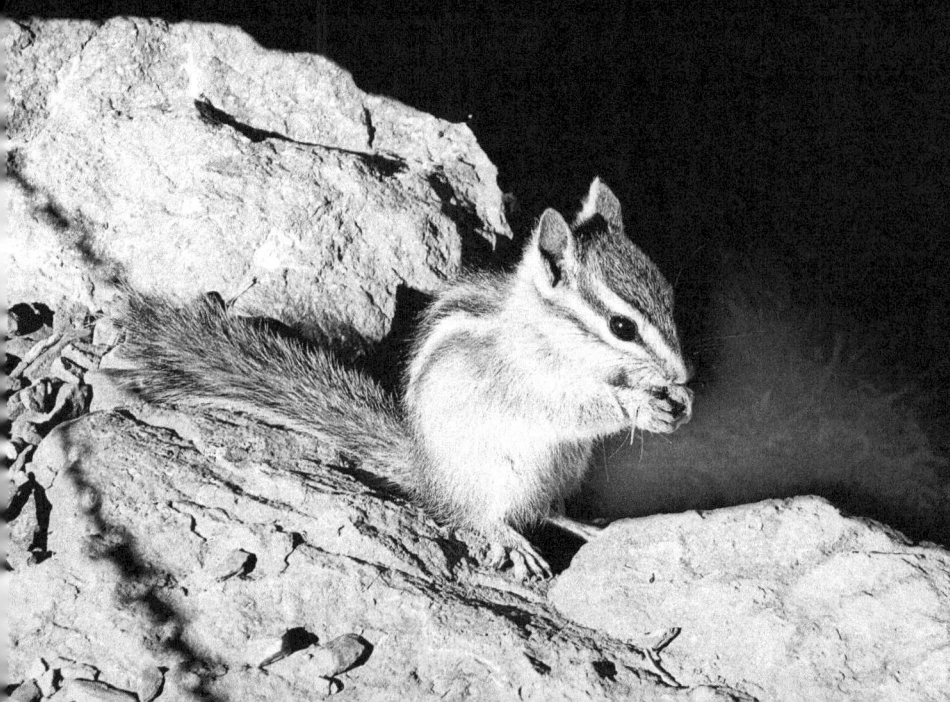

SOMETHING STIRS DEEPLY

Something stirs deeply
In the chambers of my heart,
When touched by the thought
That love and death can impart.
For with the one it is connection,
And with the other loss
Of connection with loved ones,
And even with myself.

Love opens the heart
That is yearning to feel,
While death can crack it open
From a hardened shell
And soften it through the pain
We may want to deny,
As we allow our tears to freely flow
Until they happen to run dry.

So different are these two
In how they are perceived,
For love will feel inspired
While death will be feared
Until the time it is embraced
Within the wings of Love,
Beginning its transcendence
As acceptance becomes enough.

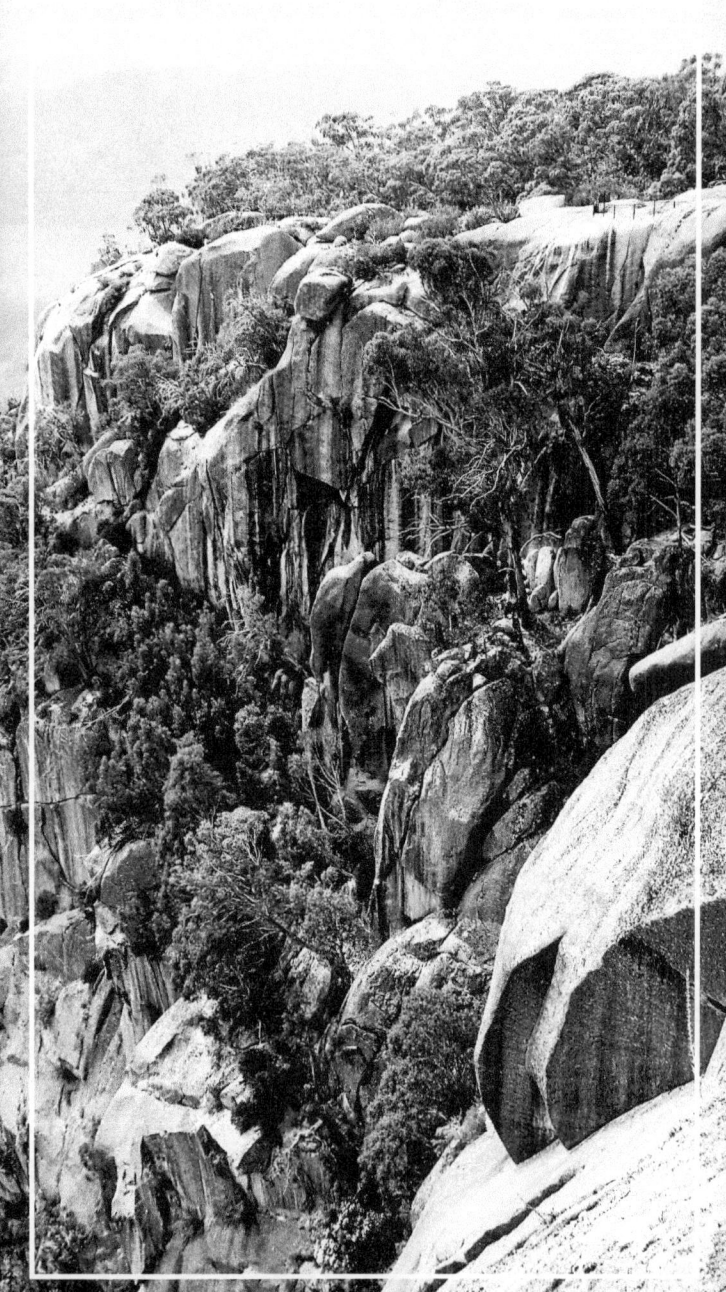

6.
Whisperings of the Heart

WHISPERS ALMOST HEARD

Whispers almost heard reside within,
Whispers that I am whole,
That Freedom is not something obtained
But arises from the Soul.

Whispers that tell me I am not the fears
That bind and limit my love;
Whispers that I am potential unbound
Beyond what I dream of.

Whispers that I need to embrace all life
As I learn to extend beyond myself;
Whisperings that I subtly sense,
Saying I am part of something else.

Whispers almost heard reside within,
Whispers that inspire me to dream
Of living from a place of authenticity,
Rather than from a place to be seen.

Whispers that faith will sustain me
In my belief within myself;
Whisperings that nothing changes,
If nothing is ever changed or felt.

Whispers that everything has a place;
Whispers that the purpose will be known,
For Life does not create the seed
If the seed was not meant to be grown!

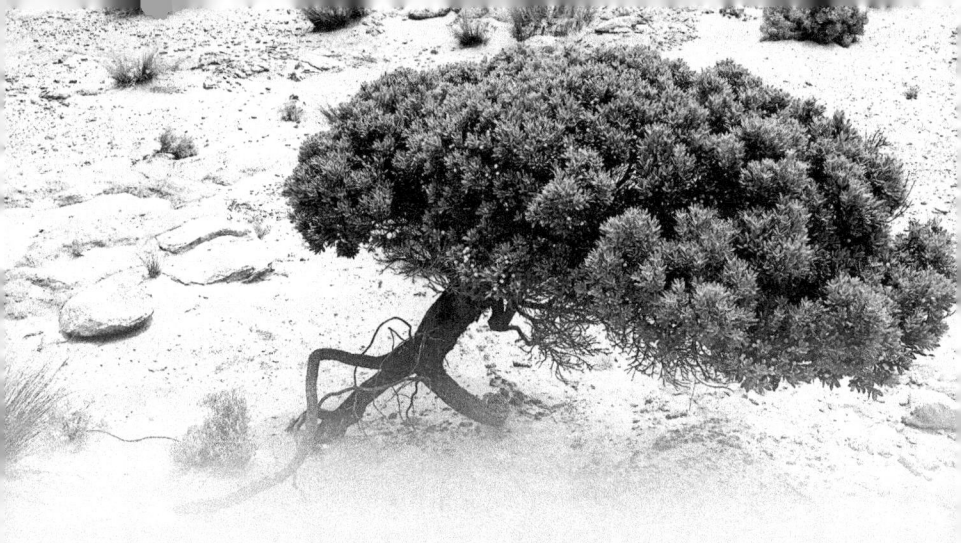

Do You Hear the Call

Do you hear the call
That comes upon the winged nights,
When dreams are played upon the field
That rests beyond your normal sight?

Do you hear the Siren's call
That draws you near with enchanting voice,
To yearn for all that may be gained
While forgetful to the cost?

Do you hear the call
That whispers for something more,
That urge to go further
Than where you've been before?
Of the feeling that is restless,
Awakening deep within
The desires of your Being,
To know what you've always been?

Do you hear the call?

BEAUTIFUL

H ow often do you rejoice
In being who you are?
Never will another be like you,
With your mixture of shades and hues
That make you so beautiful!

Your past is unique
As your future and your dreams,
Your perceptions, your beliefs,
And how you are feeling.
The conversations you have
And the challenges you face,
As the people you meet
To whom you relate.

The places you have been,
The things that you know,
Your experiences lived
And the mysteries explored.
The questions you have asked,
The doubts you have had,
Your successes and failures
Along your life path,
And the way you go about living!

As you look at life
Through the eyes of Wonder,
You will see yourself
As being truly beautiful!

THE GIFT OF LIFE

I am here pondering this gift of life,
For a gift it is
As I've only that time
Between my birth and death
To open my eyes to this mystery
Of which I am a part.

Each day
I have a chance to explore,
To express what for me is true,
To bring into being
What I need to be seeing
In the moment.

Within this gift of life
I need not achieve to feel love,
Nor succeed
To know the beauty of another soul
That stands before me.

Yet I feel my humanity
With its frailties and strengths,
And am humbled by the beauty
Of this extraordinary mystery
Of which I live.

It Is

It is in the reflection
Of a moment of beauty,
In the perception
Of what is real,
From the depth
Of our very being
That we allow
Our self to feel.

It is in the gaze
Of an infant's eyes,
Through the questions
That arise with youth,
In the faces
Of those more wizened
That tell us
What it is we knew.

It is from a need
That springs an action,
Through a thought
That all is born,
It is in our being
That we find meaning
To what was hidden
To us before.

LIFE FEELS US

This world of diversity
Is the playground of our Soul,
To know fortune and adversity,
Darkness and beauty,
And all the feelings
Which impress upon us
To show where we are.

We feel Life and Life feels us,
Sensing if we are ready
To move beyond perceptions,
Past the corridor of expectations,
To enter through another door.
One we sensed before
But that has been closed
Because we did not know
We simply needed
To untighten our fist
To open it.

This life is a gift.
In receiving it, we only need
To appreciate it.

TAKE A STEP BACK

When I cannot see beyond
   Conflicting views at hand,
I need to remind myself
That I need to once again
Take a step back,
To look with fresh eyes,
For only then can I find a way
To encompass contradictions.

If I saw from a grander view
Than the limited one I have,
I would see beyond
Things being good or bad
Or right or wrong,
For these are but judgements.

Opposites occur,
A condition of their cause.
They are but part of a whole
Based on broader laws.
So if I take a step back
To look through fresh eyes,
I might find a way
To encompass contradictions.

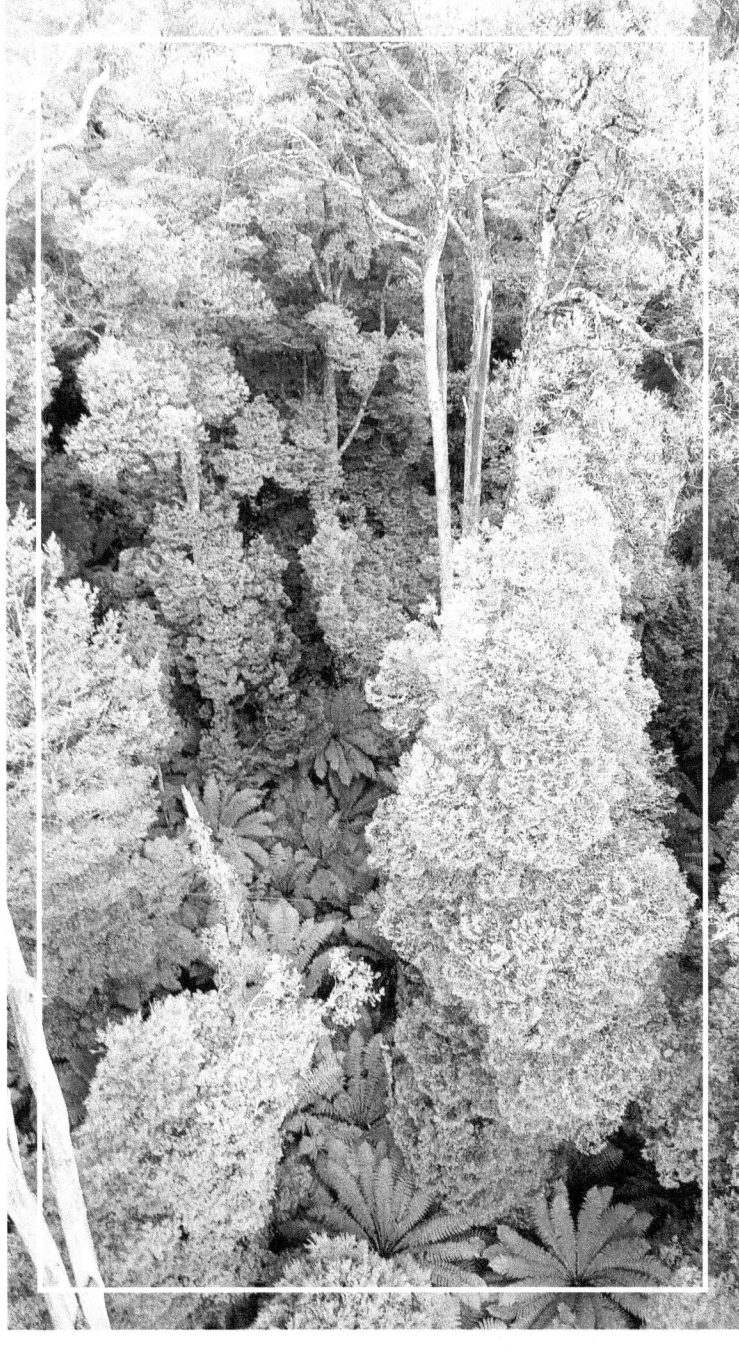

You Only Need to Be Yourself

The flower does not try its colors to hide.
The sun does not want its rays not to shine.
The bird cannot help but singing its song,
Nor will the wind attempt to stop blowing.

The tree does not mind the form it takes.
The bee will continue its honey to make.
The fish will not stop from learning to swim,
Nor the spider its web to spin.

The stream does not deny its downhill flow.
The moon does not dampen its beautiful glow.
The mountains will not hide their majestic heights,
Nor a lake imagine itself being dry.

Do you believe you need to change
To fit in, to be the same
As someone else?
You only need to be yourself.

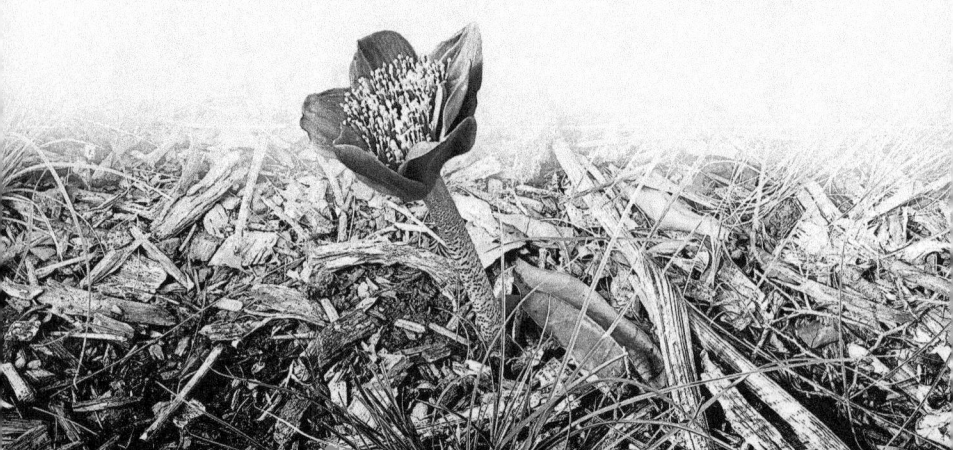

WHO WOULD TELL

Who would tell the rain
It needs to be wet,
Or how its droplets
Should glisten in the light?
Who would tell a rainbow
What colors are best for it,
Or tell the sky
To be spaciously wide?

Who would tell the dawn
To start before the day,
Or that the stars
Should glitter in the night?
Who would tell a valley
Just where it should lay,
Or the Redwood
How to reach its soaring height?

Who would tell a desert
It needs to be dry,
Or an ocean
That it should be full?
Who would tell you
To be other than you are,
For no one can be
A better you.

WHISPERINGS OF THE HEART

In the whisperings of the heart
Lie the mysteries of the Soul,
While our emotions pose the answers
To what we need to know.

And within the confines of reasoning
Are beliefs that fallow lie,
For without the desire to see what Is,
We see what is before our eyes.

As we tread our path of Awakening,
The journey will surely unfold
And encompass all that we have learned
And all there is to know.

Wisdom will then merge with Love
As we embrace where we are
From listening, yes, from listening
To those whisperings of the heart.

THE POWER OF THE HEART

As we learn to live in peace
From a point where love can start,
We become witness to
The power of the heart.

It affects our very thoughts
By changing the way we feel,
And allows the Virtues to arise
Upon the altar at which we kneel.

The pulse of Life as felt within
Is rhythmically sustained,
While the heart communicates
And brings coherence to the brain.

It soothes a restless mind
Bringing calm within the storm,
Where the scales of Reason balance
As Compassion is reborn.

As we drop into our heart
So it can breathe through us,
Life then falls into
Simple awareness.

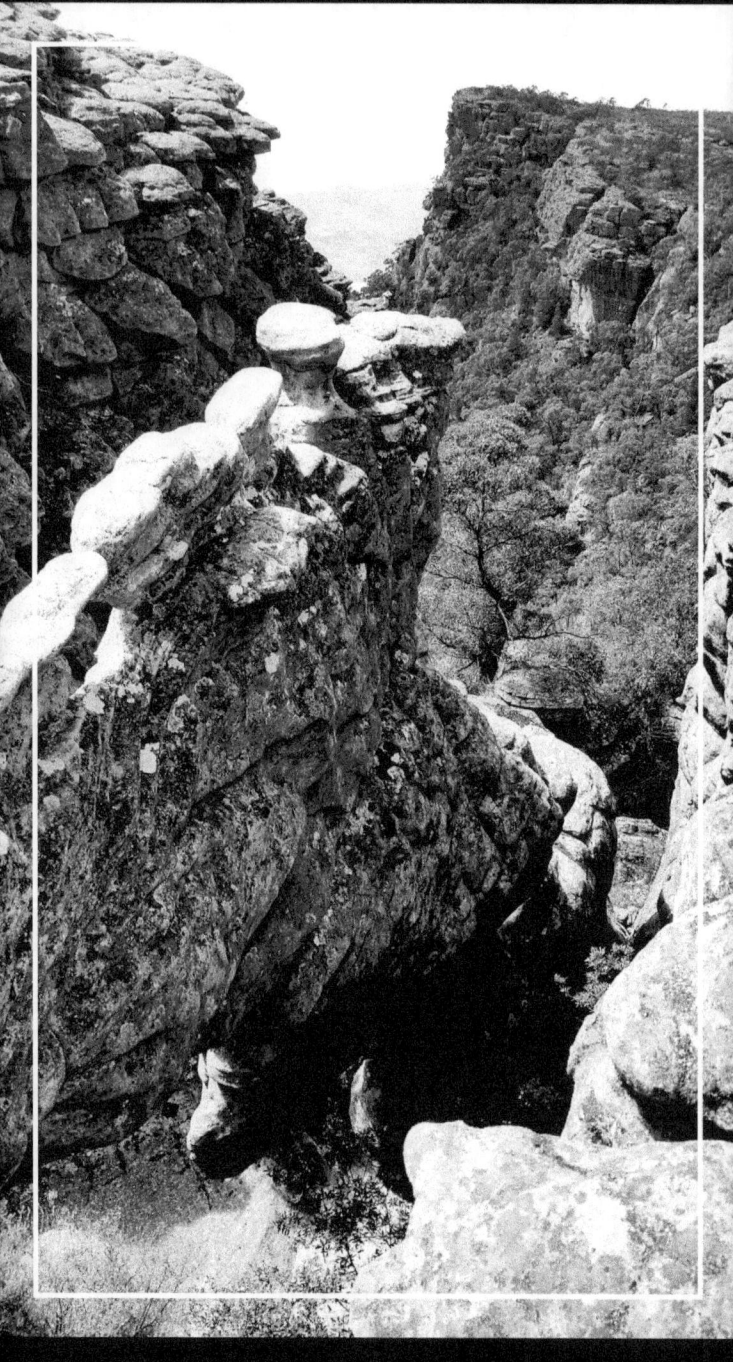

7.
Guide Me to That Place

THE SEED

You lie there
Complete
Within your simplicity.

Your form belies
The possibility
Of what you could become
Once you awaken
And unfold
Into your potential.

Within,
An image is contained,
Unseen,
Of that which is
As yet unborn ...
That which you are,
And will become.

In you,
I see something
I search for
Within myself.

WE HARVEST
WHAT WE HAVE GROWN

We harvest what we have grown.
No sprout appears
Where no seed has been sown,
And no crop will emerge to produce
The flowers that become the fruit
By which it is known.

The seeds of thought
Are scattered wide.
Many planted and tended
Over time
Become desires within the mind.

But how many thoughts
In a day do we have
That are focused on the fruit,
Not the seed we plant?

When we dig up Desire's
Emerging roots continually,
Through doubt,
Is it a wonder
That they do not sprout,
But wither?

How I Look Is What I See

How I look is what I see,
From the depths of misery
To states sublime,
From a moment of Eternity
To 'No-Time' at all.

As I try to understand,
Beliefs get in the way.
Coloring my perceptions
With emotions
That belong not to that day
But to the Past.

If only I could perceive
Through another's eyes,
My life would be governed
More through my heart,
And my actions empowered
To impart through Soul's response
The gift of Love
That heals the wounds
Of Separation.

When I am not so seduced
With how things appear,
I can see more how things are —
Intricate yet simple,
Plain yet beautiful in their Wonder.
That is the essence of Joy.

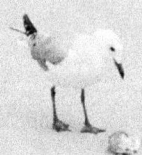

WHEN I FIND MYSELF

When I find myself
I will say hello,
For my searching takes me
Along that road
Of questioning beliefs
About who I am,
Through tortuous turns
And seemingly dead ends.
Through battles I hope
To never see again,
And of those
From which I run.

When I find myself
I will say hello,
When I reach the point
Where I can see below
The fears and wounds
That cover me,
My armor
From which I hesitatingly
Look out to see where I am.

I will say hello
When I finally meet
The one who joyfully
Greets me along the road.
The one needing not to be told
That no matter
How young or old I am,
Though I journey to Time's end,
That through my searching
I will find myself.

GUIDE ME TO THAT PLACE

You came to me to know me,
As I may know You,
Sensing into and filling me
Like a hand in a glove.

As You reflect Spirit,
I reflect You,
As I live this life with choice
To define it.

You are eternal!
You can never be defiled
Though You have merged with me,
With the Temporal,
Guiding and prompting
Along the way
This personality now displayed.

I make my choices,
Causes for Your uptake,
From which are sown
The experiences needed
As a means to gain balance.

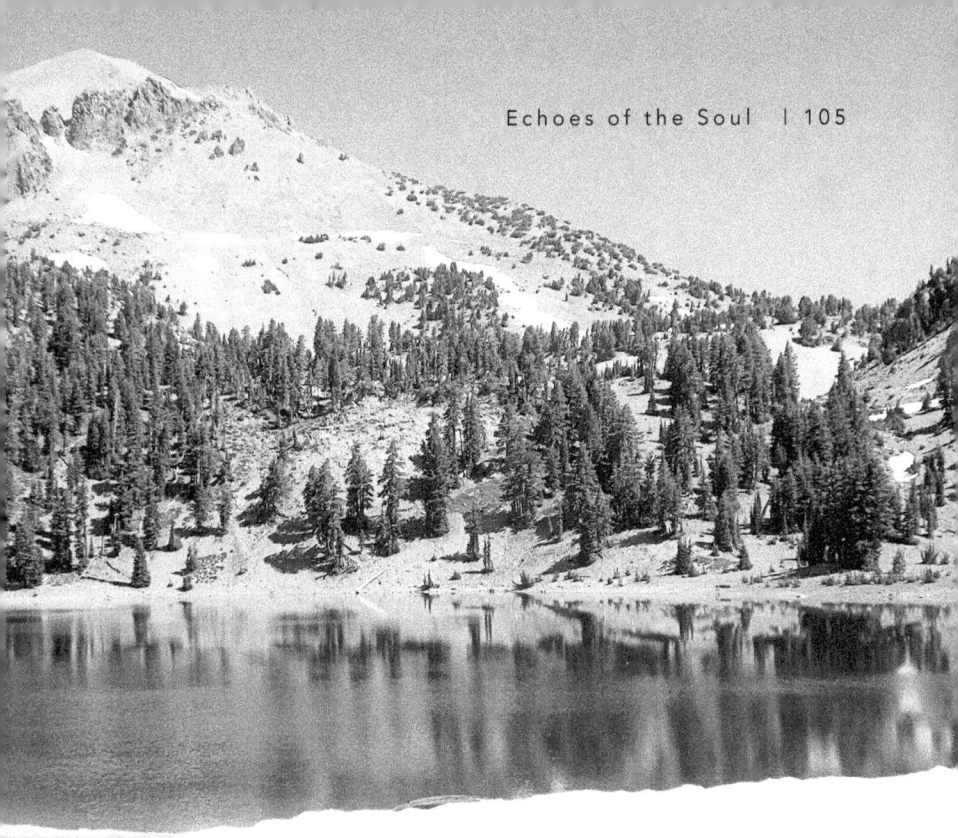

You were birthed as I,
For the Divine to experience
All parts of Self
From which to know *all*
Through which Souls grow.

Guide me there,
Guide me to that place
Where Choice and Life
Become aligned
With the Mind of the Divine!

Déjà Vu

I stand here
Feeling like I have been here
before.
It is a subtle sense
That penetrates to the core
Of my being,
Going beyond reasoning,
Yet the feeling remains.

It is not like a photograph
Or a snapshot of time
That defines this moment now.
Rather, it is a living sense
Of moments spent,
Of my having been here before.

There is a familiarity
With this landscape,
Something I cannot place
My finger upon,
Yet as real to me
As the land I stand on.

The people here greet me
In a friendly way,
Almost as if they knew me,
And though I am a stranger
It is very comforting.

Is it imagination?
I think not
For it feels too real,
This feeling I feel,
This feeling of Déjà Vu.

LUCID

I find myself aware
Within my dream world,
Awake while I am asleep,
Conscious that I have the power
To move and think
Within a dreamscape
Created by my subconscious.

What is happening here?
How does this come to be,
In these moments in which
I am freed
From the conventional reality
I live within?

Can I deny I am aware
Of being aware,
In these moments of sleep
Where I have become lucid?

Can I accept the possibility then
Of what others say,
Of what others have faced
On their own journeys
Of Awakening?

For I have heard
That Awareness
Transcends even Death ...

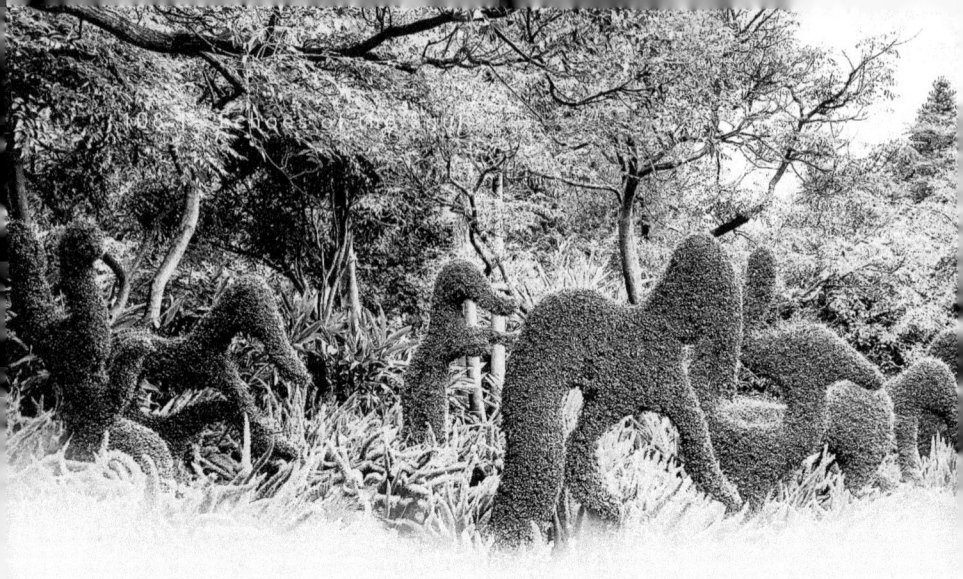

WHERE IS IT THEY GO

Where is it they go
    The dreams I once had,
Of which I often spoke
When I was young?
As I look back
Upon those early times,
I feel that yearning
From how I longed.

My life has taken me
To places I had never been,
To dream dreams I never dreamt
I would see.
And the dreams I lived
I know will remain,
Until I finally
Set them free.

IN MY DREAMS I AM FREE

In my dreams I am free!
Free of my identity,
My body, my home.
I am free to roam
And fly without constraint,
Free of the bodily aches
That pain me.

I am free of family,
My work, my car.
Free to start upon
Adventures surreal,
And free to be real
With my feelings!

I am free to be
A hero or foe.
Free of Time,
And where distance
Is not known.

I am free to dance
With moves unmarred,
On a twinkling star
In the heavens.

In my dreams I am free.
The dream state shows me
Soul's freedom realized.
It shows me how I am!
Now, I only need awaken
From the Illusion.

IMAGINE THIS WORLD

Imagine this world —
Where labels no longer define
Who we are.
Where borders and boundaries
Are erased
And conflicts faced and resolved
On the scales of Justice.

Image life lived
Without the constraints of time ...
Living more in the moment,
Less in the past,
Mindful of where we are at
As we move into the experiences
That define us.

Imagine this world —
This world of creation
Empowered by our intent,
By our desires.
Where wrongs are addressed
And our lives blessed
With peace.

Imagine how freeing it would be
To finally know.
To refine our goals,
Our very Being by realizing
The one who is behind our face.

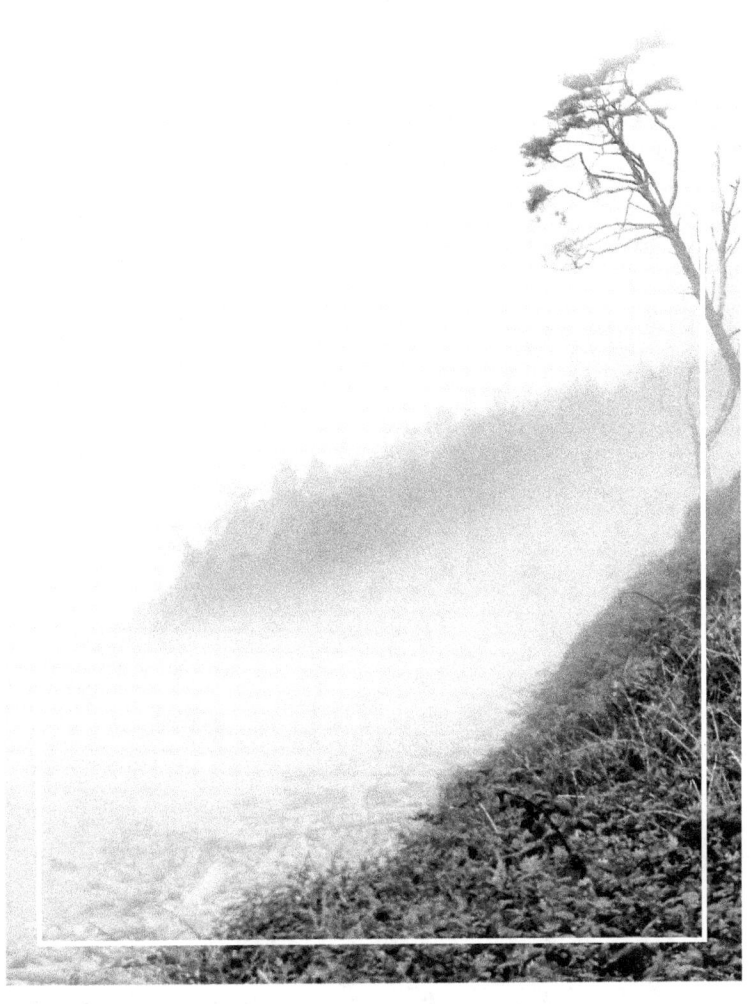

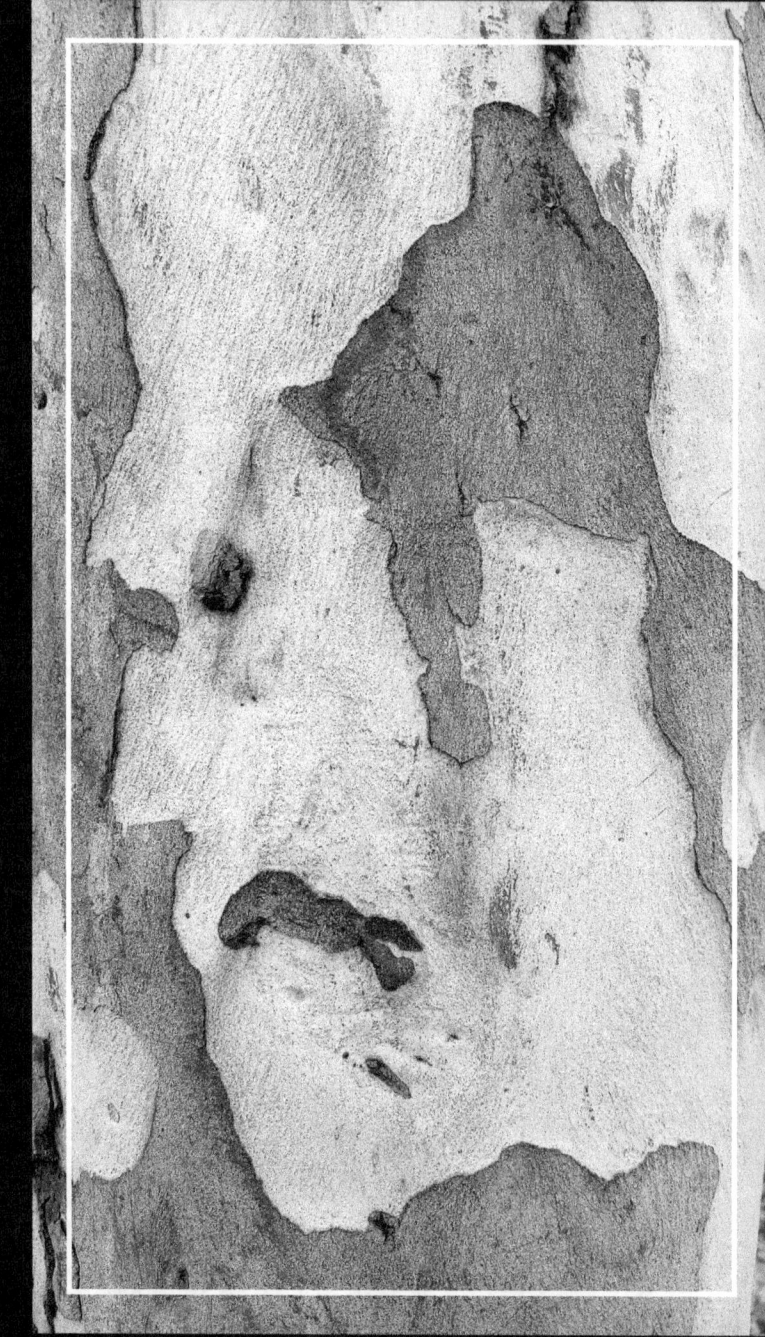

8.

Breathe Me In

THE FLOW OF LIFE

The minutes tick on,
    The hours pass by,
I am carried along
In the flow of Life.

Through eddies and rapids,
In stagnant pools darkened,
Around another bend
I am carried like flotsam.

But I have a Will,
Thus I can choose!
The flow stands not still,
Yet, I can make a move.

I can strive to make a difference,
One better if I can,
Resisting my own resistance
As part of the Plan.

As the minutes tick on
And hours pass by,
I need but determine
In the flow of Life
How I choose to be!

THE BALANCING OF SOUL

Of the flesh, of the Spirit,
A dual purpose, dual learning ...
To satisfy the yearnings
Of both worlds.

Energies masculine, feminine,
Of thought and deed,
Of bonds, desires and needs ...
Part of our growth towards Freedom.

Free will to choose,
To see how we see.
From our beliefs
We create as we need to experience,
With emotions to guide us ...
An Indicator of how we are going.

Soul growth is without limits,
But balance must occur
From all of Life's desires
Until there remains but one yearning.

Through the balancing of Soul
We become mirrors for the Divine,
Reflecting qualities
That shine from the light
Of our Becoming.

I Am Grateful

I am grateful
To be alive another day,
As I draw my breath within
And feel the blood flow in my veins.
As I follow another thought
And express it as I can,
Whether that be through words
Or some other form again.

I am grateful
For what I have learned today
That fills my life with what I need
To help me on my way.
For both the trials and tribulations
That have made me who I am,
For the dreams I hold when I'm awake
And for those when I sleep again.

I am grateful for the capacity to love,
Though at times my heart is closed ...
I am grateful for those friendships passed
And for those I may someday know.
I am grateful for this chance to be,
And to give in my own way,
And I am grateful for the night
As I am grateful for the day.

I am grateful for the beauty I see
In the various natural forms
And for the creativity
That inspired minds have borne.
I am grateful for the moments of peace
That allow me to reflect within
As I slowly come to a point
Of accepting who I am.

Yes, I am grateful
To be alive another day,
As I draw my breath within
And feel the blood flow in my veins.

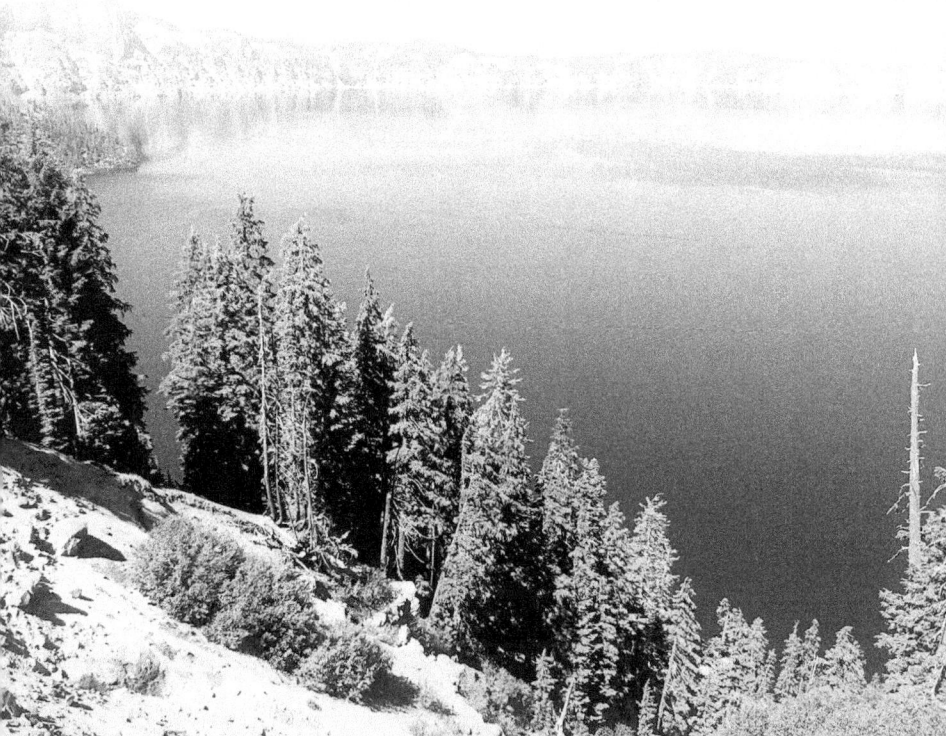

Breathe Me In

Breathe me in ...
Take all I am, all I can be,
So I may serve as part of Thee.
Breathe me out ...
Thy Mind and Will imbued with Love
Impart to me an experience of
Thy Grace that does not judge.

Breathe me in ...
All I experience is Yours again
Through eyes reflecting from within.
Breathe me out ...
I live this life until it's done
So grateful that I from You come,
Here to realize we are One.

Thy breathe of Life does deeply flow
Within all things, that much I know.
No one nor thing can separate be
From You to us or them to me.
So breathe me in and breathe me out.
Thy eternal breath is why I am now,
And forever shall I continue to be,
Part of You when You breathe me.

Breathe me in ...
Take all I am, all I can be,
So I may serve as part of Thee.
Then breathe me out ...

HOPE

I come to you in times of prayer and need.
I soothe your mind and heart
As I touch them
With the gossamer wings of Belief.

I come as you allow your resistance to subside,
As you look for the light behind the shadows
Of your struggles.

I come in your dreams, and in each step of victory
As you pursue your own life path,
No matter how slow or fast those steps are taken.

I am that feeling, that surge of joy
That uplifts your Soul, helping you carry on
With the task of carrying on.

You breathe Me in with upturned eyes
And gladdened heart
As a place of calm arises within your mind.

You see Me in moistened eyes,
In prayerful lips,
In the focus that settles within a look
That shows others I am with you.

Some things are not meant to be.
A grander purpose cannot be seen
Until time unfolds to show you
Whether the path you wish to go upon
Is the path upon which you need to go.

LOVE

Let Me expand your heart
To reach beyond yourself,
So you can become One with Me
In the infinite joy of Being.

I will guide you to bear your Soul
As the flower bears its petals
Towards the sun.
I am that yearning
To lose yourself within another
And to find the other within yourself.

I am in your dreams of Beauty,
In the joy of Wonder
And the promise of Hope.

I am there in the sunset
And in the sunrise,
In the valley depths
And in the mountain heights.
I am within the deserts
And in the expansive seas,
Whenever you look for Me.

Embrace Me, for with Me
You are free to fly unrestrained,
To know as you need to once again
That you and I are One.

COMPASSION

I am there
In those moments of selfless care
Towards another,
Feeling for the pain of the other,
Drawn by the yearning to know
Through the whisperings of your Soul
How to be of service.

You see Me in those
Who are there to help.
You feel Me
When assistance is heartfelt,
And although you may forget,
Even then know that
I am also there for you.

I am there when you weep
From that feeling forlorn,
And when you question whether Justice
Is equal for all that are born.

When you feel Me,
You will be moved to assist,
Finding your own way to resist
The urge for complacency.

Take My hand, and I will lead you
Within your heart of Light,
To see beyond the thinning Veil
Into the eyes of Love Divine!

MY ANCIENT MOTHER

I feel the warmth of your embrace
As you hold me near.
In the wild open spaces,
I feel you there,
Comforting me, comforting me ...
My Ancient Mother.

I see the glow of your smile
Reflected in the sky,
In the colors that are found
As the sunset arrives,
And you comfort me, you comfort me ...
My Ancient Mother.

I hold my breath in joy
From being there with you,
As you teach me
About Love and Beauty too
While comforting me, comforting me ...
My Ancient Mother.

As Silence sings its songs
I know I am blessed,
For in you I find
A place where I can rest
As you comfort me, comfort me ...
My Ancient Mother.

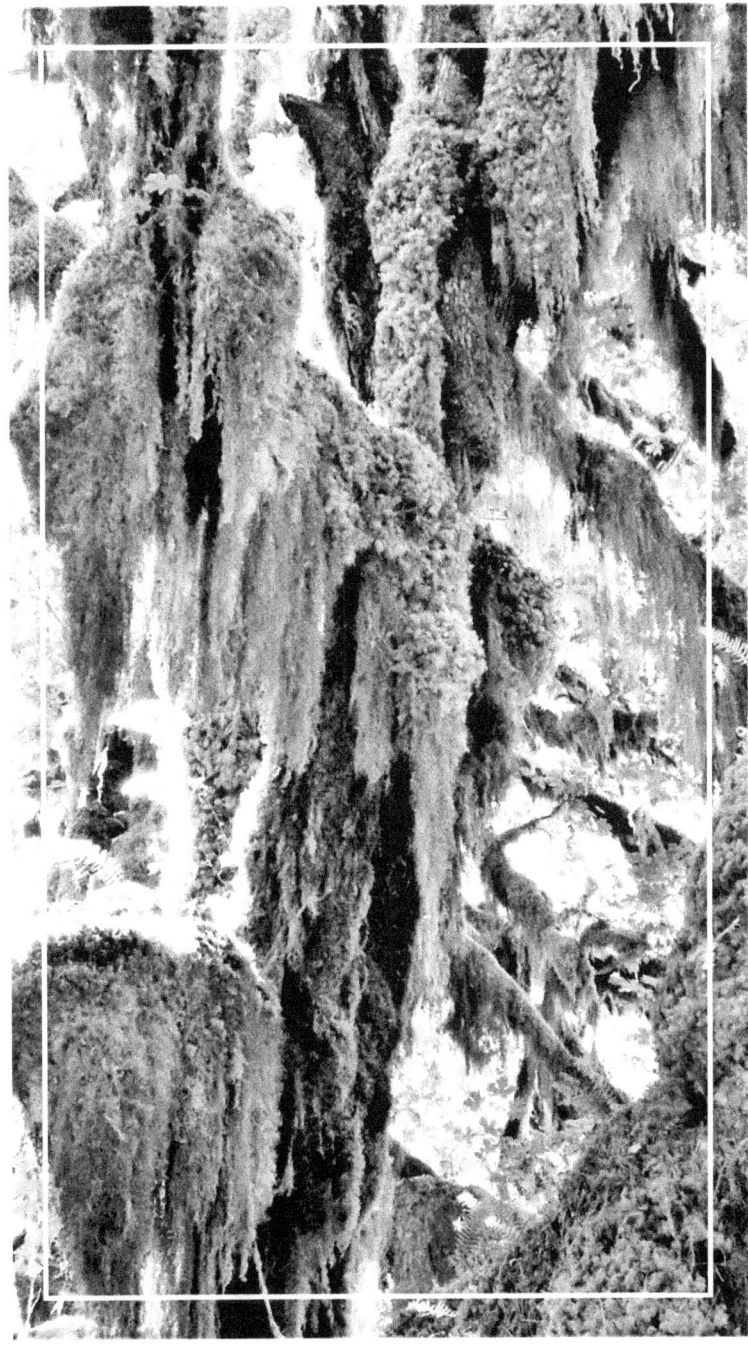

Oh, Wondrous Moments of Joyous Beauty

Oh, wondrous moments of joyous Beauty,
Lift Thy veil that I may see
Thy face radiant with the light of Love.
Dance with me this dance of life unrestrained,
With heart and soul exposed,
Unfettered by the deepening mysteries
From which You arise.

Let me hold Thee close to me,
Forever a remembrance of the light
That shines through when You smile.
In those moments where darkened clouds
Confuse my sight,
Take my hand and lead me to that place
Where I can rest within Your embrace.

Oh, wondrous moments of joyous Beauty,
What am I without Thee?

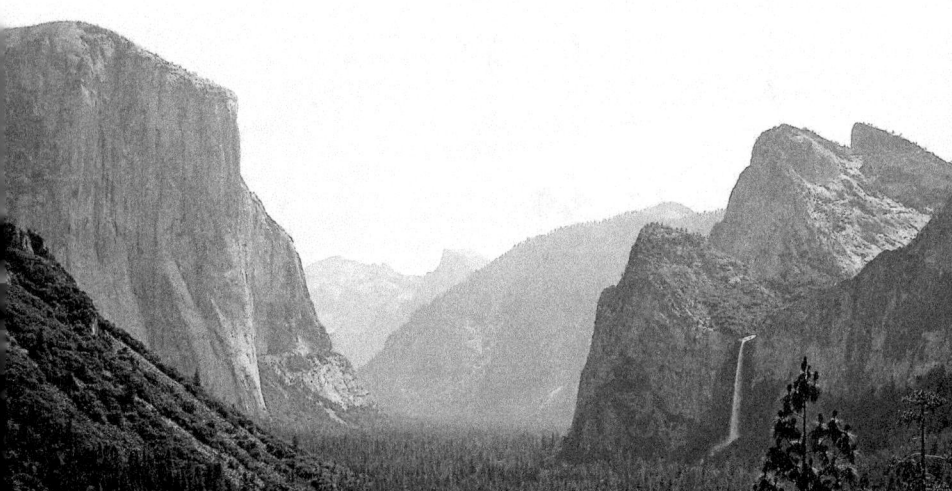

LOVE REFUSES NO LOVER

The ocean refuses no river
Wanting to merge into its depths
As it courses from its origins
To reach where it can rest.

The sky refuses no bird
Taking wing to be in it,
Where it finds a different freedom
And a way of expressing it.

The mountains refuse no climber
Attempting to climb its slopes,
Who face its challenges with courage
As they embark upon the unknown.

The volcano refuses no stirrings
That are welling from below,
Though they be changed forever
As part of its fiery flow.

And Love refuses no lover
Who is willing to feel with their heart,
Awaiting the time of their yearning
For Love to play its part.

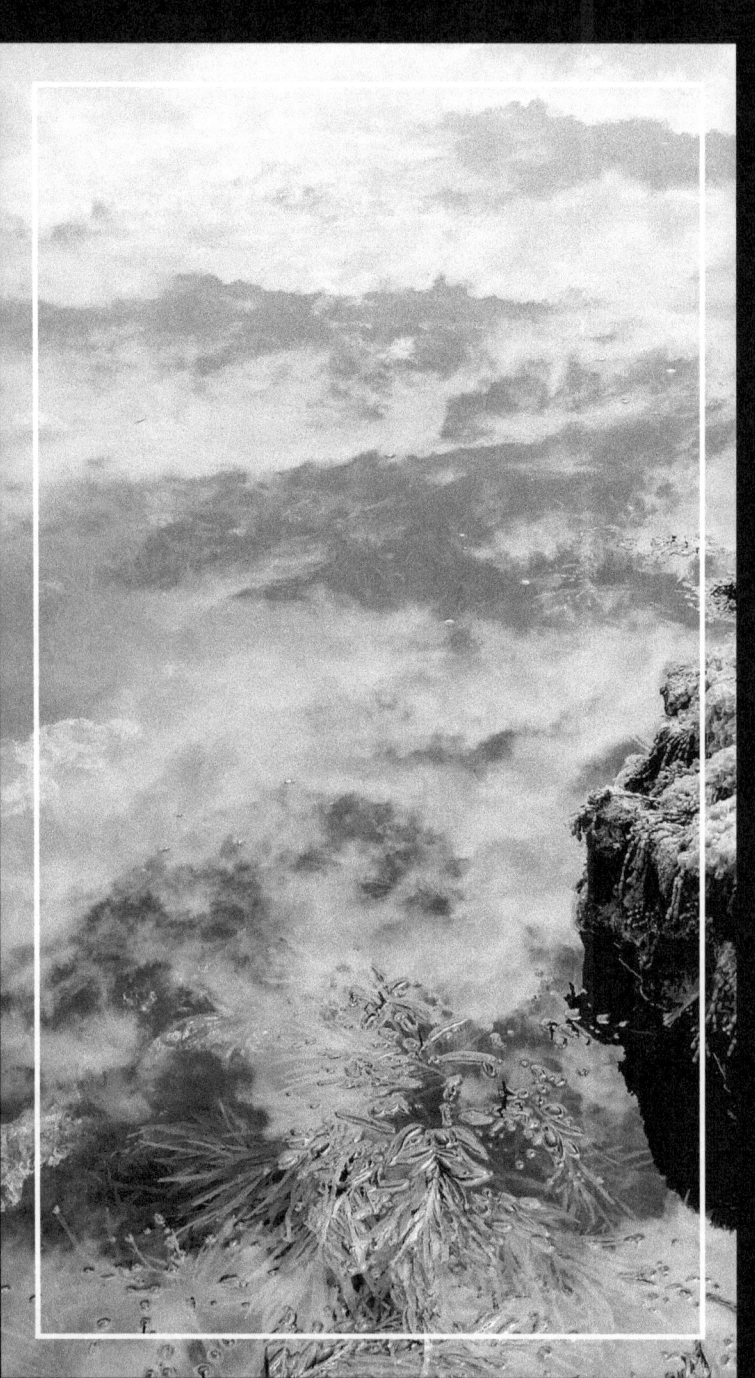

9.
Echoes of the Soul

When I Look
I Know You Are There
All the Years I Have Lived
Echoes of the Soul
As I Sense the Loss of Myself
The Response
In the Mind of the Divine
With Different Eyes
The Gift
A Different Way of Seeing
Speak Through My Heart

WHEN I LOOK

When I look at the sky,
I see Your eyes
Looking down upon me,
Deep and loving,
And it leaves me believing
In the infiniteness of space
Within ourselves.

When I look at the
Sharply etched mountains,
I see Your features
Etched within them,
And I know that forever
Shall we have the strength
To become.

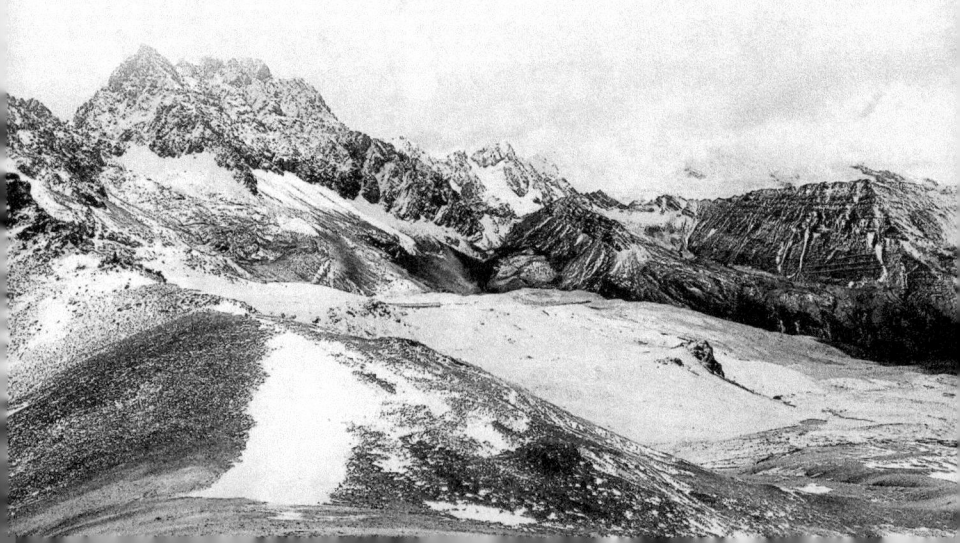

When I look upon
The woodland lakes,
I feel the quiet beating
Of Your heart,
And I sense
The tranquil reflection
Of nature's beauty
That rests within us.

When I look
At the meadows
Splashed with the color
Of flowers,
It reminds me
Of the radiance of light
That shines through
When You smile.

When I look around me,
I see You there,
Close to me,
And my heart rejoices
In the blessing
Of Your love.

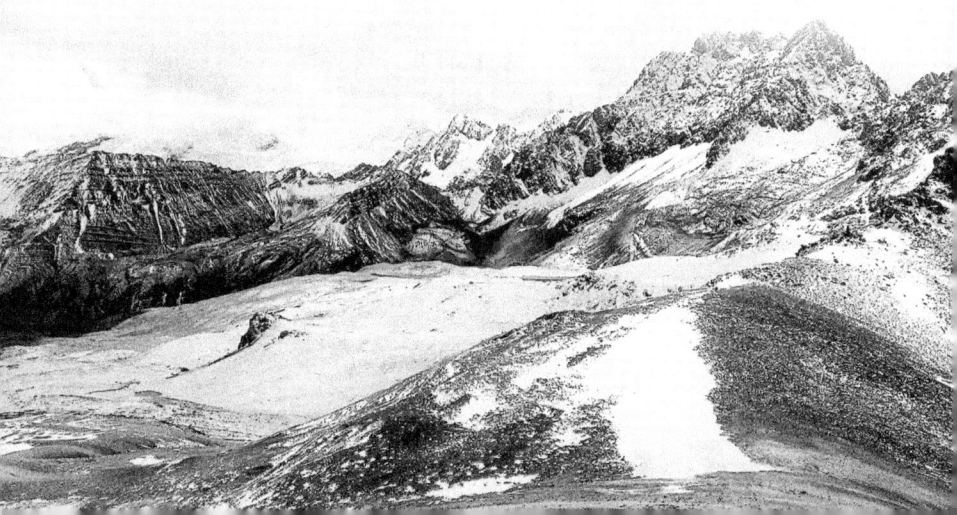

I Know You Are There

I know You are there
As a whisper in my heart,
As a sigh upon my lips,
And a reflection in my thoughts.
As a yearning in my Soul,
As the feeling of being fair,
As my breath is to me ...
I know You are there.

I know You are there
From the song on the breeze,
From the look between lovers,
And the movement of the seas.
From the echoes of laughter,
From the Joy that brings tears,
As my thoughts are part of me ...
I know You are there.

I know You are there
Through the birth of a child,
Through the journey of our lives,
And the answers we have found.
In the feeling that inspires,
Through the moments shared,
As my heart beats within ...
I know You are there.

ALL THE YEARS I HAVE LIVED

All the years I have lived
Have brought me to 'Today'.
They have brought me to this time,
To this place I am now,
So that I might find within
What I need to find without.

All the years I have lived
Becoming who I am,
Have shown me to myself,
This one I choose to be,
So that I can say 'I lived Life,
And that Life lived me'.

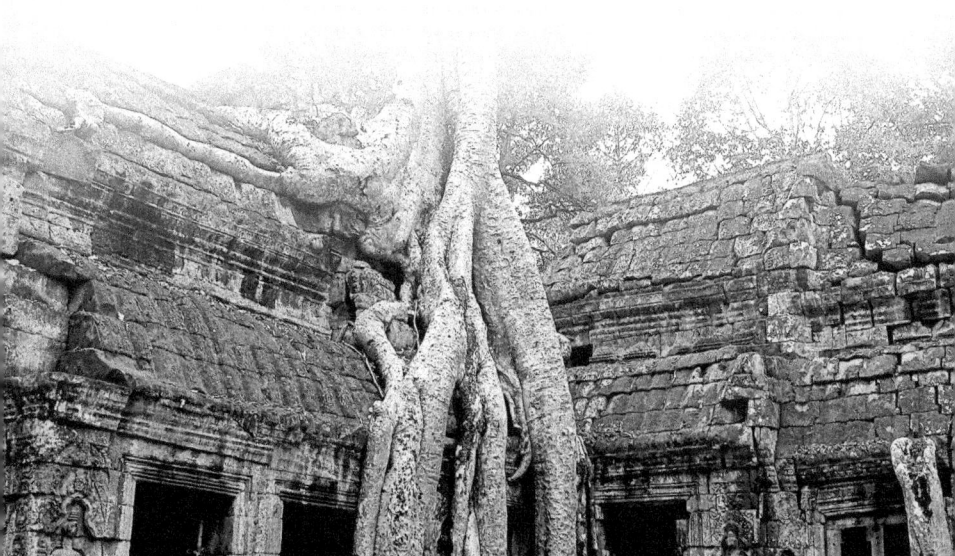

ECHOES OF THE SOUL

Hear Me whisper through your heart,
For that is how you feel Me,
That is how you sense Me,
That is how you know I am with you.

I am your immortal Self
Grounded in time, in you,
Though timeless and unchanging am I.
I am here to experience through you
How you see your Self
And to remind you in moments of selflessness
How you really are.

I know this body of blood and bone,
Of mind and ego too,
And I wait as we journey throughout
The days and years
For you to listen and respond to my prodding.

To remember that I am you,
As the formless through form,
That you may awaken to the illusion of form
As but a distraction.

You sense my presence within,
Knowing something deeper is real
That feels eternal.
It is Love!
Listen to these whisperings,
These echoes of the Soul.

AS I SENSE THE LOSS OF MYSELF

Terror arises as I sense
The loss of my sense of self,
As I start to fall into the abyss
Of the Unknown.

My heart is beating so hard
It feels like it wants to burst out
Of my chest,
And my mind is thrown into confusion.
My Being screams and I want to flee,
But something, something tells me
Not to resist.

My eyes are closed
And I am withdrawing further within,
Witnessing my own implosion.
I am being sucked into a void,
And I fear insanity or death awaits me.

I find it hard to breathe.
Amidst this terror, this confusion,
A thought arises ...
"If I am to die, then so be it.
I can do nothing now but surrender."

As I let go of my resistance
To letting go of what is known,
Of my very identity,
I begin to feel the fear diminish.
Surrendering to the Unknown,
I become a witness to the experience
Of my Being.

THE RESPONSE

L ord, tell me why we are here
And if You really care.
Do You ever yearn to be fulfilled
Or even seek to express Yourself?

Do You have any desires,
And do we in Your eyes really matter?
What response might You give,
For I know not what to think of it!

I Seek, I Yearn, and I Desire —
But only for your happiness here.

My Seeking is only to express Myself
Through the hearts of all when Love is felt,
And My Yearning is only for your gain
To find Me through your searching.

You are not yet aware
I created you for My Joy to share.
But you are given a will to choose
What you seek and what you do.

Know every choice will have a cost
In what is gained or what is lost,
And that ephemeral things will not last
In your search for happiness.

You seek a Truth you know inside,
One from which you cannot hide,
For in Love's quest by your yearning Soul,
It is I that you seek to know.

So I patiently wait for you to learn
And find 'I Am That' which you truly yearn.
Then My Love within you will recognize
I am also the Love you see in the eyes
Of all others.

IN THE MIND OF THE DIVINE

Angels appeared and celestial Beings.
I was shown other worlds within other
dreams.
I saw the Heavens in their glory sublime
And states of Being impossible to define.

Why I am was to me shown,
And a vision of the infinite Cosmos
As I journeyed along the Spiral of Life
And stood before Wisdom's watchful eye.

I witnessed how Life unfolds our growth
And know each of us are exquisite Souls
Come to fulfill as only we can
The part we play in fulfilling the Plan.

I heard Love's voice, and know it to be true
That our lives unfold as they are meant to,
That the trials and tribulations we find
Further Love's plan in the Mind of the Divine.

WITH DIFFERENT EYES

I see the world with different eyes
From that I had before,
For now I see the beauty that lays
Beyond Perception's door.

For as my gaze was cast within
And my heart became aligned,
My Soul came into communion with
The Mind of the Divine.

My heart burst forth its gratitude
As Love was allowed to expand.
I saw Death but as a change of guards,
And felt it as my friend.

Life flowed before my view
In constant changing forms,
And finally I knew that I knew
Why I had been born.

I felt so full of gratitude
And knew I had been blessed,
For now Life I understood
In ways words cannot attest.

I see the world with different eyes
From that I had before,
For now I see the beauty that lies
Beyond Perception's door.

THE GIFT

What is this gift that was received
That has touched me so deeply?
I know I have profoundly been blessed
By the touch of Grace at Love's bequest.

A calling came forth for me to heed
With the release of Love's energies,
A gift that has changed my life
Through what it is I realized.

My heart was opened and I allowed
Myself to face the fear somehow
Of impending death, of the Unknown,
Through which I had to go alone.

Now I say I am at peace
For I know Life just strives to be
And is One within the varied forms
From that One they are varied born.

Love now beckons as my guiding light,
However I find it as I live my life,
For the Gift bestowed that was received
Blessed and deeply touched me.

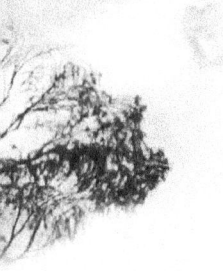

A Different
Way of Seeing

There's a different way of Seeing,
A different way of Being,
A different way of living
In the world.

One where there is no
Questioning
Of the way to be,
Or what can be achieved.
And there is no believing,
For there is no need
When the need to believe
Is limiting.

When mind is not limited
To the need to try,
When sight is not limited
To what lies outside,
There will be a different way
Of Seeing,
One defined by our Being.

When our vision,
When our perceptions are clear,
Our Knowing will set us free.

SPEAK THROUGH MY HEART

Speak through my heart
That I may hear You
With my Being,
That I do not forget
Thy voice,
Thy voice that whispers
Unto me, calling me,
Calling me.

Though my steps falter,
Guide me to that place
From which You beckon,
That I may find You
And realize that You
Have been with me always.

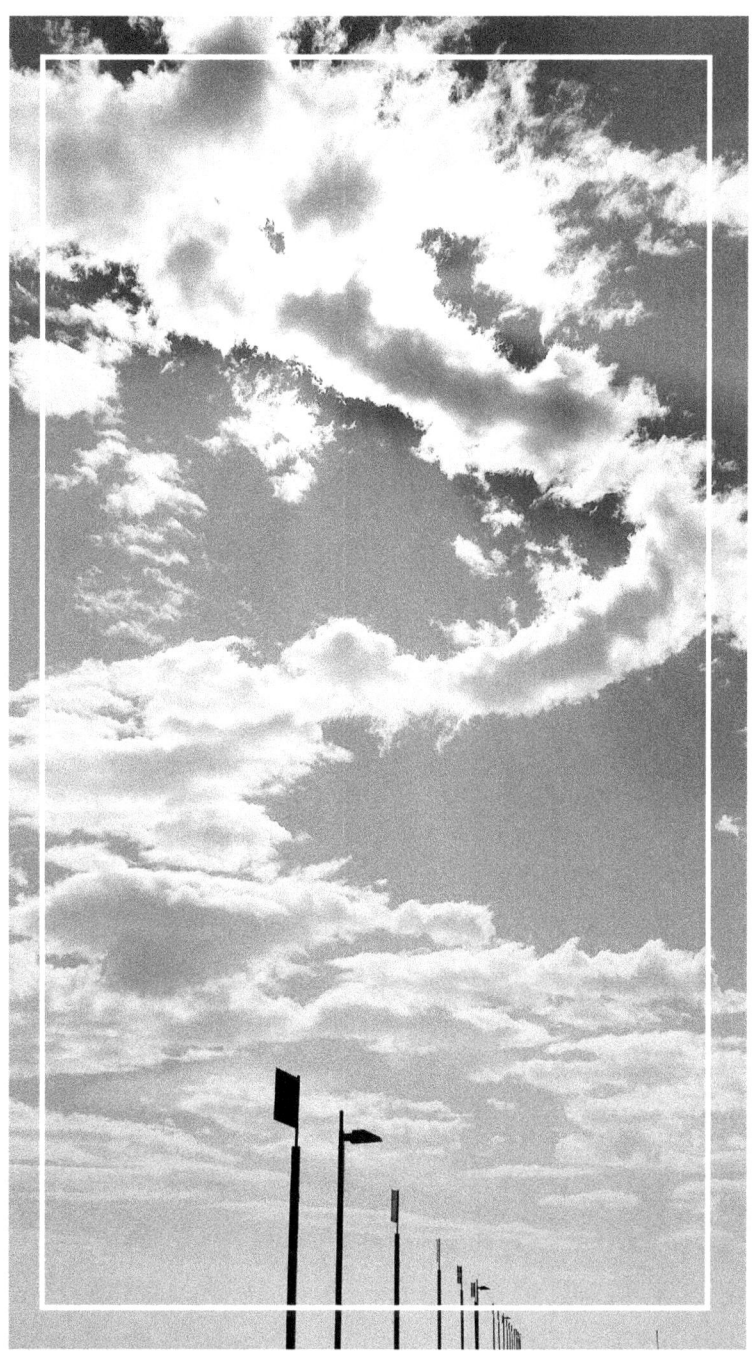

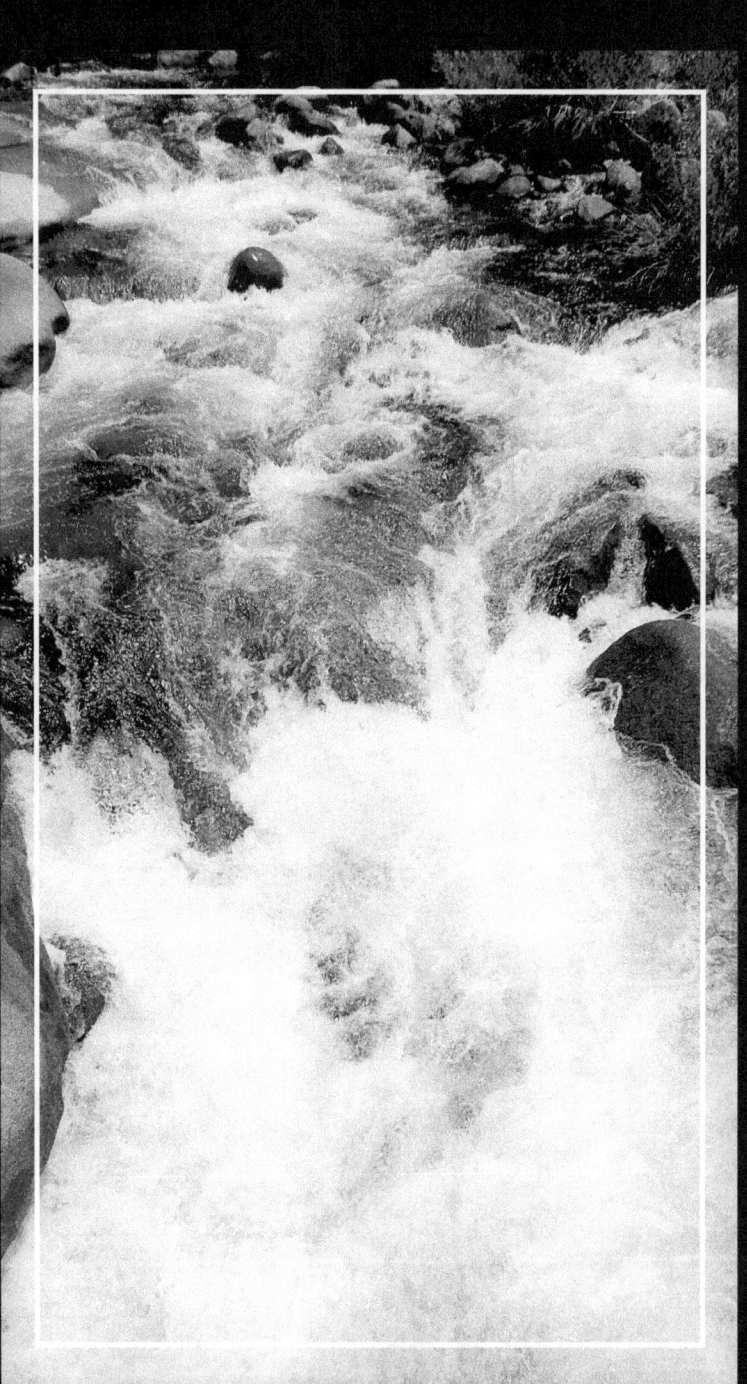

10.

I Hear My Soul Calling

If I Look at My Life
When My Time Is Done
With Whom I Think I Am
Help Me to Surrender
I Hear My Soul Calling
Lift Up Your Eyes
The Ocean Wave
Remembering Who I Really Am
Back, Back Again

IF I LOOK AT MY LIFE

If I look at my life
Focused upon my goals,
I miss the flow
That is the journey
Of never-ending learnings.

I can look at the things I did,
Accomplishments fulfilled,
But how I was, how I lived,
Was it real?

Lessons not learned
Will be there for me
To complete.
After I have a chance to rest,
Will I choose them to repeat?

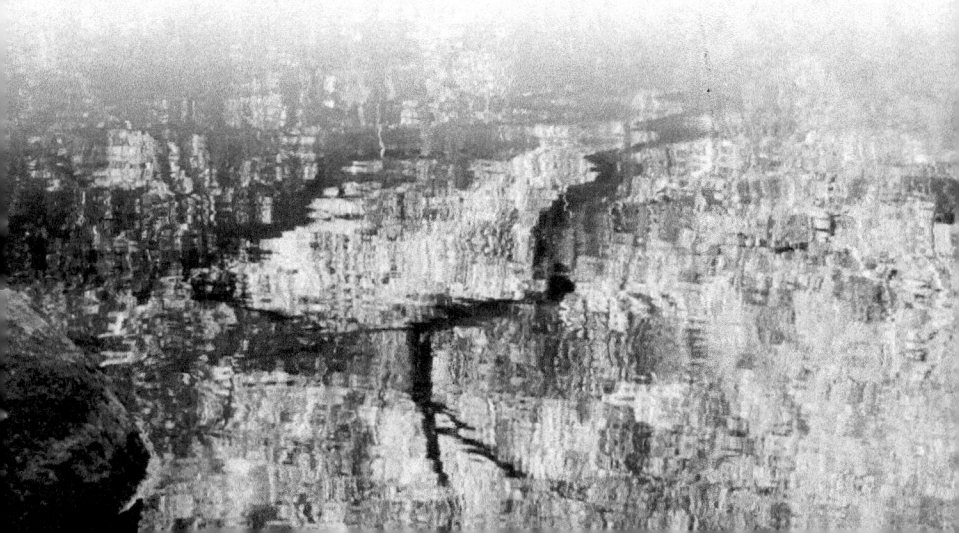

WHEN MY TIME IS DONE

When my time is done,
And I can do no more,
Will I be satisfied
With what has gone before?
Will I look upon my life
Content in how I lived,
When my time is done
And I have nothing left to give?

When my time is done
And I rest my weary feet,
Will I feel gratitude
Arise within to meet me?
Will I feel at that time
That finally I am free,
When my time is done
And I have nowhere left to be?

When my time is done
And I must say goodbye,
Will I welcome with open arms
The other side of Life?
Will I have a sense of Peace
With whom I am that day,
When my time is done
And I am on my way?

WITH WHOM I THINK I AM

I should not be surprised
To be told I am going to die,
For death is just the final Act
Of this play I call my life,
But still the shock of being told
Has struck that note within,
Where primal fears run hand-in-hand
With whom I think I am.

It is hard for me to imagine
A time when I am not,
For I embraced
This part that I got
With the Acts I played
And the characters I have been,
That has defined this life
With whom I think I am.

I fought with my anger,
My denial, and my shame,
Feeling I could have done more
If I lived this life again.
But the initial shock has settled
And I carry on as I can,
Coming to a greater peace
With whom I think I am.

I look through different eyes
Than those I had before.
I am no longer interested
In evening out the score,
For my time is more precious now
Than it has ever been,
As I connect more deeply
With whom I think I am.

HELP ME TO SURRENDER

Help me to surrender
Unto what I cannot comprehend.
To surrender my resistance,
To embrace You once again
So that I may live in Love,
Mindful of my days,
That I may learn to love Life
In all of its display.

Help me to surrender,
To feel that release
That comes with acceptance,
That will bring to me peace.
For as I live my days
Trying to remember,
My memory of You
Will come as I surrender.

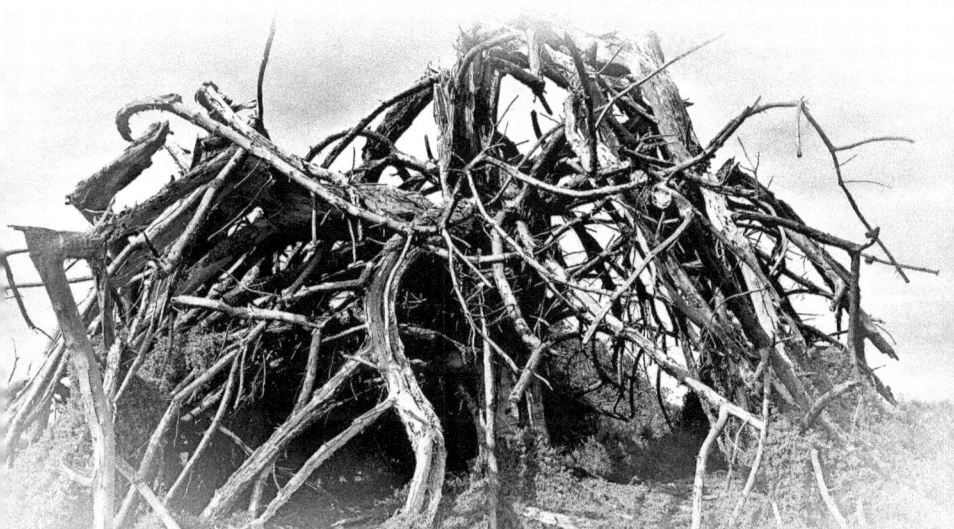

I Hear My Soul Calling

I hear my Soul calling.
It does not speak to me in words.
It is like a felt presence
Where feeling and thought merge.
It is a sensing within my Being
That it is time to go home,
To let go of my luggage
So I am freer to roam.

I know I must let everything go —
My memories, my things,
And this body I know.
For another adventure awaits me
Just beyond my sight,
Once I have finished
This grand dance of Life.

I have tried in my own way
To do what I can,
To become who I could,
To learn my lessons.
Now my time has drawn near
With these breaths, my last,
It is time to let go
Of my future and past.

I hear my soul calling,
Now it is ringing a bell.
It has turned off a light,
Something is different I can tell.
My vision grows dimmer
But I hear laughter in the air
As loved ones start to gather
To greet me over there.

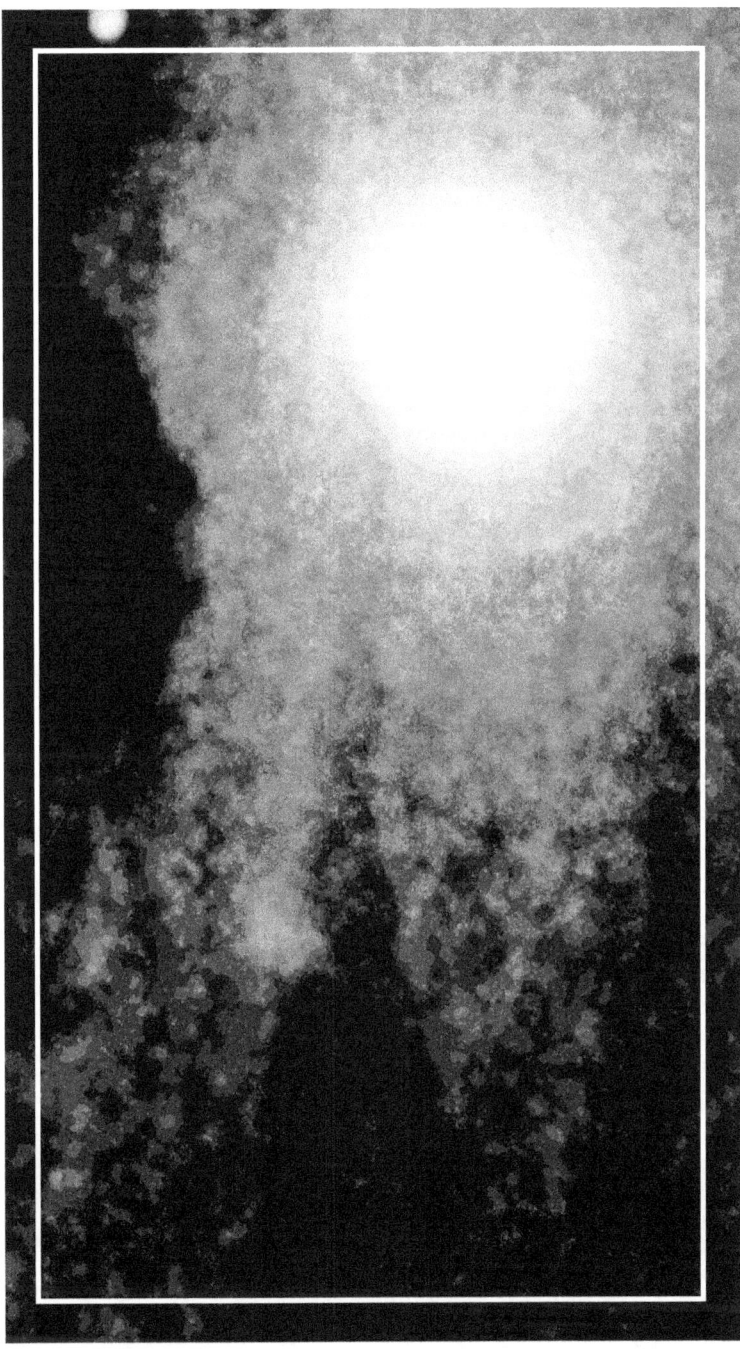

LIFT UP YOUR EYES

L ift up your eyes, my child,
Lift up your eyes,
And see that glimpse of light
That beckons you
Unto its embrace!

Lift up your eyes
And recognize the face of Love
Who calls you,
Who will take you by the hand
And walk alongside.

Lift up your eyes, my child,
And know that Love is but
A breath and a heartbeat away.

THE OCEAN WAVE

I was watching a wave come in
As I stood upon the sand.
It seemed to rise momentarily
And then subside again.

Another wave took the place
Of the one that had been before.
After a succession of waves
One finally reached the shore.

Each wave arose to its height
From the body of water below.
There was a time for each to be —
And a time for each to go.

The wave feared not for its loss
When its time had finally come,
For though its form had disappeared
It became part of the vast ocean.

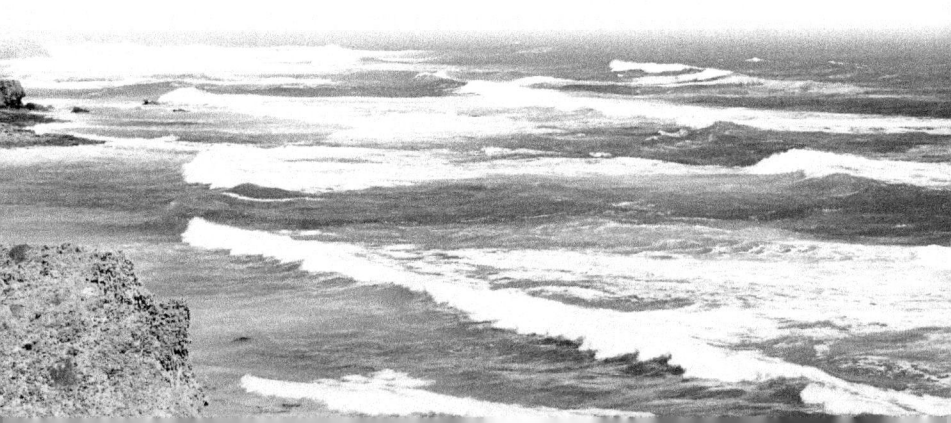

Remembering Who
I Really Am

I look upon this scene
Of moistened eyes and ended dreams,
Of muted voices of those in mourn
For the one now gone,
Who rests in peace,
The one whom I recognize
Had been me.

How can I console
When I cannot be seen?
I know I must leave this gathering,
That it is time,
Yet I am not sad
As I now find I am free.

I am released from worry
And no longer doubt.
Now it is clear —
I chose to forget when I came here
So I might live life afresh,
Remembering who I really am.

BACK, BACK AGAIN

The Soul stood before The Maker
And was asked,
"And what did you learn
On your earthly sojourn?"

And the returning Soul replied,

"I experienced pain and sorrow,
Anger, doubt, and fear,
And learned lessons do not come easily
While I struggle.

I knew peace and happiness,
Made friendships short and long,
And saw the power of Love transform
The lives of those it touched.

I witnessed the seasons change,
And travelled the world
To find people were the same.

I toiled the fields,
Climbed majestic mountains,
And felt the caress of the breeze
On my face.

I competed, conquered,
Was defeated, and tried again.
I questioned why I was there,
Why things were as they were.

Then from within, an answer came.

'I am here to grow in love,
To become aware,
To know my life is my creation
With all its joys and pain,
Until such time I realize who I am.'"

The Maker smiled and said,
"You have learnt well.
And where would you like to go now?"

"Back, back again!" said the Soul.

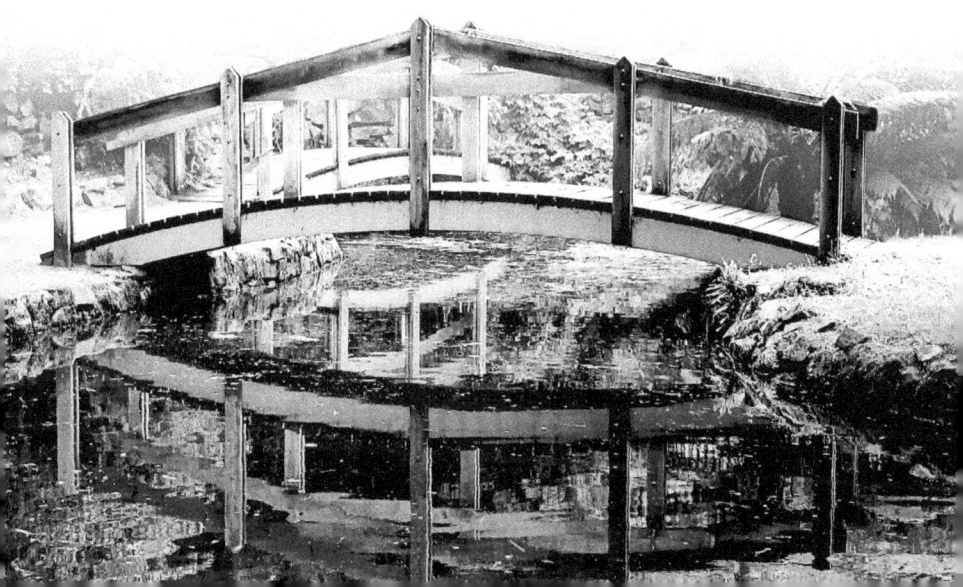

About the Author

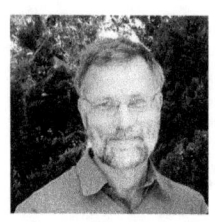

Bennie L. Hannah was born in Merced, California, and grew up in the nearby city of Turlock. Since he was about 16 years old, he has had a deepening interest in the area of spirituality, science, metaphysical studies, and poetry. His travels have allowed him to experienced many different cultures around the world, which have helped to shape and reinforce his world view that 'All are One'.

Bennie worked for the U.S. Forest Service in California while undergoing his Bachelor's Degree in Natural Resources Management at California Polytechnic State University, San Luis Obispo. Shortly thereafter, he joined the U.S. Peace Corps in Nepal as a Forestry Volunteer and later returned for a short period as a Forestry Trainer.

Afterward, he returned to San Luis Obispo to do his Master's Degree in International Agricultural Development before moving to Frankston, Australia, where he currently lives. He worked for the City of Melbourne, Victoria for 18 years, before being retrenched. It was during this introspective period that he reconnected with the writings from his youth and began writing again.

Bennie started working for a Community Development organization in The Greater City of Dandenong, Victoria. It was during this period that all but one of the selections within this book were written.

He is an avid hiker and bush walker. He has two sons.